Creative Ideas For Lent

edited by Linda S. Davidson

CREATIVE IDEAS FOR LENT, VOLUME 3
edited by Linda S. Davidson

Copyright © 1996
Educational Ministries, Inc.

Printed in the United States of America. All rights reserved. Portions of the book may be reproduced for educational purposes only. Call the publisher for persmission.

Cover design by Terry Schultz

ISBN 1-877871-93-1

Educational Ministries, Inc.
165 Plaza Dr.
Prescott, AZ 86303
800-221-0910

CONTENTS

INTRODUCTION 5

SECTION ONE—ALL CHURCH 7

    Guess Who's Coming To Worship? —*by H. Michael Brewer* 9

    John...Mary—*by Carolyn McDowell* 15

    Palm Sunday, From Palm Branches to Easter Lilies—*by Susan Gregg-Schroeder* ... 16

    Liturgy Of The Passion—*by Gwen Drake* 17

    Shrove Tuesday Traditions—*by Ann Bateman* 19

    Purim—Reading Of Esther—*by Christie L. Jenkins* 21

    The Darkening Service—*by Denise Krebs* 23

    Tenebrae Journey... Past And Present—*by Carolyn McDowell* 27

    Maundy Thursday—*by Ann Bateman* 30

    The Confession—*by Carolyn McDowell* 31

    Good Friday, Service Of Remembrance—*by Maren Tirabassi* 33

    The Way Of The Cross—*by Delia Halverson* 35

    Good Friday Vigil—*by Maren Tirabassi* 37

    Good Friday Silence And Poetry—*by David Trembley* 39

    Holy Saturday, Communion Meditation—*by Joyce DeToni-Hill* 41

    Lent And Easter Packets—*by Deborah Payden* 42

    The Questions Of Mark—*by Robert G. Davidson* 43

    A Blossoming Cross —*by Mary Jo Shannon* 48

    Readings For Lent—*by Ann Wiggins* 49

    An Abstinence Game For The Family—*by Christie L. Jenkins* 50

    Telling Stories During Lent—*by Elaine Ward* 51

    Stones—*by Don Hartman* 54

    Symbols Of Holy Week—*by Elaine M. Ward* 55

SECTION TWO—CHILDREN 57

    A Lenten Learning Center—*by Peter Olsen* 59

    Word Find—*Ann Bateman* 60

Lent: A Time For Listening—*by Joanne Wilson* *61*
Release Butterflies—*by Delia Halverson* *62*
Lenten Symbols Banner —*by Carolyn Egolf* *63*
New Life—*by Jane Maehr*. *64*
All God's Children—*by Jane Maehr* *65*
Waxed Onions—*by Delia Halverson* *66*
A Walk Through Holy Week—*by Penny Lowes* *67*
Lenten Puzzler—*by Ellen Humbert* *70*
He Has Risen! —*by Joyce DeToni-Hill* *71*
Easter Lilies—*by Linda Bloomgren* *72*
Lenten Cross—*by Deborah Payden* *72*
Palm Sunday Echo Pantomime—*by Deborah Payden* *73*
Easter Egg Art Project—*by Teresa Baggot* *74*
Plant A Sign For Christ—*by Virginia Fleishans* *74*

SECTION THREE—YOUTH 75

Understanding Death—*by Elaine M. Ward* *77*
Lent: Not Death But Renewed Life—*by Terry Deffenbaugh* *80*
A Lenten Journey—*by Deborah Payden* *83*
Lenten Steps—*by Miriam Perry* *85*
Litany For Lent—*by Carolyn Egolf* *90*
Easter Acrostic—*by Carolyn Egolf* *90*
Infamous Traitor—*by Joanne Wilson* *91*
Good Friday Newspaper—*by Deborah Payden* *93*
Easter Dawn Youth Service—*by Dallas Brauninger* *95*
Resurrection Rap—*by Deborah Payden* *98*
Personalities Of The Passion—*by Carolyn Egolf* *98*
Lenten Feelings—*by Joanne Wilson* *99*
Back To Jerusalem—*by Carolyn Egolf* *106*
The Pretzel—*by Christie L. Jenkins* *109*

About the Authors 111

INTRODUCTION

We have been most gratified to hear of the many complimentary remarks regarding our **Creative Ideas for Lent** series. So many of you have called and written to thank us for publishing these helpful resources. That encourages us to do more, so here is our latest effort.

In this volume we present more ideas to assist you as you plan the Lenten season at your church. This volume includes more worship ideas than the others ranging from a hand washing service to a Seder meal. There is a Tenebrae service, a Good Friday journey, and even a Holy Saturday meditation.

If you are looking for all church events, you will find many ideas to involve all ages. Have a fun Shrove Tuesday celebration for everyone. Or plan a Lenten journey for the six weeks of Lent using a different symbol each week to emphasize an important part of the Lenten story. Or put together Lenten packets for each family of your congregation to use at home. Or make a Lenten devotional for the 40 days of Lent using scriptures or original writings by members of your congregation.

There are lots of crafts and activities for children. Help them make banners, plant bulbs, bake cookies and decorate eggs as they learn the significance of this special season. You never know what seeds will take root with children as you try to convey God's love.

Have your youth work on a Holy Week or Good Friday newspaper to get a feel for life in biblical times. Who were the characters involved in the events of Holy Week? What circumstances led them to Jesus? Why couldn't they help him escape death? Or offer them a Seder meal to help them understand the Jewish tradition. Or have your youth plan an Easter sunrise service for your congregation. Perhaps one of the many plays included in this volume could be presented.

Let these ideas ignite a spark in your creative planning for Lent. May they aid you to tell this important story about our Lord, Jesus Christ.

Section One
All Church

Guess Who's Coming To Worship?

by H. Michael Brewer

Our worship committee decided to combine two ideas in order to enrich our Lenten season. First, we made plans for a "reverse Advent wreath." In a prominent place in our worship space we arranged a cluster of seven purple candles and one white in holders of various sizes and designs. To symbolize the suffering and rejection of Christ, we successively quenched one purple candle each Sunday through Lent and on Maundy Thursday. The white Christ candle was extinguished on Good Friday, and rekindled on Easter morning.

But how could we work the candle dousing into the service in a dramatic way? We decided to have a visit each Sunday from some biblical character who had a personal encounter with Jesus Christ. As minister I agreed to preach a sermon based on that particular character. The possibilities were many, but we settled on a mix of themes and genders represented by the bent woman (Luke 13:10-17), the Gadarene demoniac (Luke 8:26-39), the woman with a flow of blood (Mark 5:24b-34), the rich young ruler (Mark 10:17-22), the woman at the well (John 4:7-30), the paralytic at Bethesda (John 5:1-18), the woman taken in adultery (John 8:2-11), Simon of Cyrene (Mark 15:21), and Mary Magdalene (John 20:1-18).

The worship committee carefully selected role-players with a flair for drama. One member of the committee was chosen to serve as the costumer. Each player received their script a week early and was asked to memorize their lines.

The basic presentation followed the same outline each week. After opening announcements and prelude music, the visiting character knocked on the door, entered the sanctuary, and asked permission to address the congregation. The character spoke briefly of their experience with Jesus and extinguished one candle. Then the liturgist led a Prayer of Confession which explored the theme raised by the visitor. The Assurance of Pardon was declared by the character. Following a hymn of praise, the visitor read the Scripture lesson which told the story of that character. The Scripture lesson was carefully and minimally edited in order to make the reading sound like a first person story recounted by the character. Usually this involved little more than changing "he/she" to "I". After the Scripture reading the actor left the sanctuary, changed clothes, and re-entered through the rear doors for the remainder of the service.

The weekly visits generated enthusiastic conversation around the coffee pot, added drama to our worship, and brought the Scriptures to life for all generations. And the progressive quenching of the candles offered a vivid reminder of our Lord's passion and approaching death as we journeyed through Lent. Our worship committee has already decided to repeat this idea next year with different characters!

Following are the scripts for each service.

THE FIRST SUNDAY IN LENT —THE BENT WOMAN

(The Bent Woman comes in leaning on a cane and is severely stooped. Slowly the Bent Woman makes her way to the area in front of the Communion Table.)

Bent Woman: You would not know me by name, but you may have heard my story. I used to walk like this. For eighteen years I was stooped over. People stared and pointed at me. Children chased me and called me "the bent woman." I could not stand up straight or look another person in the eye.

Then I met Jesus. Now I walk like this. *(Slowly she straightens up.)* I don't need this anymore. *(She lays the walking stick at the foot of the Communion Table.)*

Jesus set me free, and there were those who hated him for it. They said he was evil because he healed me on the Sabbath. *(She snuffs one purple candle.)* I don't understand all the laws in the Bible, but I know Jesus wasn't evil. It was not an evil man who made me stand up straight again.

THE CONFESSION OF SIN *(led by liturgist)*:

Leader: Healer of the oppressed: We are not so different from the bent woman. We, too, are burdened down by quarrels left smoldering, unspoken apologies, mistakes we should have set right.

People: Christ, lift us up!

Leader: We are bowed down by guilt: lukewarm in our discipleship, scarcely moved by the needs of others, ignorant of the Scriptures that ought to guide our lives.

People: Christ, unburden us!

Leader: We are bent beneath the weight of the wrongs we shouldn't have done and the good things we have left undone.

People: Christ, help us to stand up unashamed!

Leader: Savior of the oppressed and bound, only you can straighten us out. Make us well from the sin that cripples us, and lift up our faces so that we may praise you and serve you with upright hearts.

People: Amen.

THE ASSURANCE OF PARDON:

Bent Woman: When Christ laid his hands on me, I stood up and I saw that he was smiling at me. Christ is smiling at you, too. There is no burden he cannot lift from your shoulders. Believe me when I tell you this good news. In Jesus Christ, we are forgiven.

THE SECOND SUNDAY IN LENT— THE DEMONIAC

(The Demoniac, draped in ropes and chains, enters the sanctuary with confidence and looks the place over.)

Demoniac: They used to call me Legion because there was a whole legion of demons living in me. People feared and hated me. They tried to tie me up, but I escaped and lived in a burial ground, just the demons and the dead and me. I ran naked under the sky and beat my body against the stones. There was no peace for me, and no hope.

Until the Nazarene came. He is the power of God. With a few words he drove the demons away and gave me back my life. *(The Demoniac lays the chains and ropes on the Communion Table.)* He set me free.

When the people in those parts heard that I was healed, they came in a mob and begged Jesus to go away. They ran him off. *(Snuffs one purple candle.)* Some people are more comfortable with demons than with God.

THE CONFESSION OF SIN *(led by liturgist)*:

Leader: Seeker of the lost, sometimes we choose to live in a lonely place. We turn away those who are different.

People: We shun the ones who make us uncomfortable: the ones with troubled emotions, the ones who cry out, the ones who don't fit in, the ones who wrestle demons within.

Leader: We run away from those who might have been our friends. We don't want help, or commitments, or obligations. We want to be left alone.

People: We even try to turn You away, God, but You won't leave us to ourselves. You come to our hiding place among the dead.

Leader: O God of mercy, forgive us our fear of love, our rejection of intimacy, our denial of brothers and sisters.

People: In the name of Christ, save us from the tombs of loneliness. Amen.

THE ASSURANCE OF PARDON

Demoniac: Once I was among the dead; but now the Son of God has made me alive. What he has done for me, he can do for you. In his power we are made whole! In his love we are set free!

THE THIRD SUNDAY IN LENT— THE SUFFERING WOMAN

Suffering Woman: Twelve years I was sick! Can you believe it? Hemorrhages for twelve years. I went to the best doctors. Did I get any relief? Sure, they relieved me of my life savings. I was worse off after they treated me! Hah! Don't talk to me about doctors!

Then I heard Rabbi Jesus was in town. I just knew he could make me well, but I was too shy to ask him. My illness wasn't the kind you talk about in public. So I sneaked up behind the Rabbi in the crowd, and when he wasn't looking I touched the hem of his robe.

And I got well! Just like that! *(Snaps fingers.)* I think there's nothing he couldn't do if he wanted to! It's a funny thing, though. A few days later he made a visit to his own hometown, and his old neighbors made fun of him. *(Snuff one candle.)* Even Rabbi Jesus couldn't do any mighty works there where nobody believed in him.

But I believe in him! You better believe that I believe!

THE CONFESSION OF SIN *(led by liturgist)*:

Leader: Savior of the lost: where shall we put our faith?
People: We will put our faith in our good health, our money, our insurance policies, our job security.
Leader: God forgive us!
People: We will rely on technology most high. Science will save us from hunger and sickness, grief and death.
Leader: Christ have mercy!
People: We trust the Big Stick to protect us! More laws! More guns! More prisons!
Leader: Lord preserve us!
Unison: Gracious God, we thank You for doctors and nurses, for scientists and researchers, for law-makers and law-enforcers, for every helper along the way. But teach us where to entrust our hearts. Show us where to take refuge. Lead us to our only salvation, in the name of Jesus. Amen.

THE ASSURANCE OF PARDON:

Suffering Woman: Why do we wait until all else has failed us before we turn to our Savior? Come now to the only one who can save and forgive you. Believe this good news I tell you. Put your trust in Rabbi Jesus, and he will make you whole!

THE FOURTH SUNDAY IN LENT— THE RICH YOUNG RULER

Rich Young Ruler: People have always envied me. I'm young, healthy, rich, respected. I've got it all. But it feels like something is missing. It seems like there ought to be more to life. So I went to see the Nazarene Teacher, to ask him what I was doing wrong.

"Teacher," I said. "I've always kept the laws of Moses, but I'm not happy. There must be something else."

Jesus stared at me for a long time with a gentle look in his eyes, and then—Get this now!—and then he said, "Sell everything, give away your money, and come follow me."

But I didn't give everything away, and I didn't follow him. *(Snuff one candle.)* What do I need with some crazy Teacher from Nazareth? Like I told you, I've got it all!

THE CONFESSION OF SIN *(led by liturgist)*:

Unison: Good Teacher, teach us what really matters. Teach us to distinguish between the priceless and worthless. It is so easy to love the wrong things, so tempting to chase the cheap prize, so hard to love you most of all. Forgive us for being such slow learners. May we let go of everything that gets in the way of following you, so that we may have it all through you. Amen.

THE ASSURANCE OF PARDON:

Rich Young Ruler: When the Teacher looked at me, he looked at me with love. He didn't care what I had or didn't have. He loved me for myself. And he loves you. In that great love the Teacher invites us to start fresh. Believe this good news. In the love of Jesus our sins are forgiven.

THE FIFTH SUNDAY IN LENT— THE WOMAN AT THE WELL

Woman At The Well: There was a stranger sitting by the well one day and he asked me for a drink. I saw he was a Jew, but we started talking. He wasn't like the other men I've known. I got the feeling he really cared how I felt and what I thought. He actually listened to me, instead of just waiting for his turn to talk. I forgot all about getting him a drink from the well. When I look back I think maybe I was thirstier than he was that day.

After a while his disciples came back, and I could tell they didn't like their teacher talking to a woman like me. They were worried about his reputation. I had only spent a few minutes with him, but I felt like I knew Jesus better than they did. They were supposed to be his closest friends. *(Snuff one candle.)* But they didn't understand him at all.

THE CONFESSION OF SIN *(led by liturgist)*:

Leader: Love one another. That's what you told us to do, Lord.

People: But we hoard our love because we're always wondering, What's in it for me? It's safer to love ourselves than to love each other.

Leader: You told us to love our enemies.

People: We hold back our love because we're afraid of being used. We can't let anyone take advantage of us! It's so risky to let others get close to us.

Leader: You told us to love God.

People: We try to love, but we're really not very good at it. Maybe we need more practice. Be patient with us, Lord. Keep loving us, and maybe we'll get the hang of it.

Leader: Amen.

THE ASSURANCE OF PARDON:

Woman At The Well: This is what I learned from Jesus. God loves us whether we deserve it or not. When we fail to love others, God's love forgives us. And when we learn to love as God loves, then we won't need forgiving anymore.

THE SIXTH SUNDAY IN LENT— THE PARALYTIC

Paralytic: For almost forty years I could not walk, not a step. I used to lie with many other sick people next to the pool of Bethesda. Sometimes the water would tremble as if an angel were present, and we believed that the first person into the pool would be healed. I don't know if it was true or not. Since I could not walk, I was never first into the water and I knew I never would be.

Then one day Jesus came along. He told me to pick up my pallet and walk, and I did! I just stood up! It was like nothing you ever saw. And it was like nothing the Pharisees had ever seen. They were angry that Jesus claimed to have the power of God and yet he was healing on the Sabbath. So the religious leaders decided to kill Jesus. *(Snuff one purple candle.)* Because he told me to carry my pallet, they made him carry the cross.

THE CONFESSION OF SIN *(led by liturgist)*:

Unison: Great Physician, you offer us new life, but we cling fearfully to our comfortable miseries. You want us to mount up with wings of eagles, but we huddle on our pallets. It is not your power that fails us, but our reluctance that fails you. We feel trapped in our circumstances, caged by our habits, squeezed by our limits, and we give up hope. When you call us to our feet, may we have the faith to stand. When you invite us to be well, may we have the will to change. When you challenge us to be whole, may we be brave enough to walk with you to new and better places. Amen.

THE ASSURANCE OF PARDON:

Paralytic: Do you want to get well? Take what Christ wants to give you! You want forgiveness? It's yours! You want new life? Unwrap it! You want tomorrow to be better than today? Then believe in the power of Jesus Christ, and start walking!

MAUNDY THURSDAY—
THE WOMAN TAKEN IN ADULTERY

The Woman: You can't imagine what it was like to be pulled from the house and dragged like an animal to the courtyard of the Temple, where they put me on display and publicly condemned me for adultery.

The Temple is a crowded, busy place. I felt like there were a thousand eyes staring at me, a thousand fingers pointing at me, a thousand tongues whispering about me. I wanted to die. And I guess I would have if it had not been for Jesus.

I remember it so clearly: how smug the Pharisees looked; Jesus doodling in the dirt with his finger; how he outwitted the Pharisees and made them look shabby in the eyes of the people. And I remember how angry the Pharisees were in the end.

Jesus saved my life *(snuff the last purple candle)* but it cost him his own life.

THE CONFESSION OF SIN *(led by liturgist)*:

Leader: Gracious Savior, we so often feel guilty and ashamed. We feel unworthy and unclean. When our guilt is well-deserved, we ask you to forgive us and help us to change how we are living. When we are ashamed without good reason, remind us how precious we are in your eyes and set us free from unhealthy self-condemnation. Let us live in your joy, relying on your grace, and following in your footsteps. Amen.

THE ASSURANCE OF PARDON:

The Woman: What I remember most vividly was the way Jesus looked at me after everyone else had drifted away, and the sound of his voice as he said, "I don't condemn you. Go on your way, and don't sin anymore." Jesus has come into the world not to condemn us, but to set us free from guilt and shame. Believe this! Jesus Christ has forgiven you! Now, don't sin anymore!

GOOD FRIDAY—
SIMON OF CYRENE

Simon: My name is Simon. I come from Cyrene in North Africa, what you would call Libya. I am a worshiper of the God of Israel, and so I had traveled a great distance to Jerusalem in order to celebrate the Passover in the Holy City.

While walking down the street on Friday, I saw a crowd gathered around some spectacle and I went to see what was happening. Some wretched criminal was being taken to execution. The back of his robe was caked with blood and his face was bruised and swollen. He was supposed to be carrying a cross, but he had fallen beneath its weight and now he was struggling to get back to his feet.

Suddenly, one of the Roman soldiers grabbed me by the arm and shoved me toward the fallen man. He forced me to carry the criminal's cross! But here is the strange thing. As I took the heavy timber from his shoulder the man looked up at me, and his lips moved. He was already half dead and I couldn't hear him very well. But I could swear he said, "I'm sorry." He apologized to me. In that moment I decided that I would carry that cross to the end of the world and back again for that man.

THE CONFESSION OF SIN *(led by liturgist)*:

Leader: We will begin our prayer in silence, as each of us opens our heart to God. *(After at least one full minute of silence the Leader will pray the following prayer aloud.)*

Leader: Lord Jesus Christ, who bore our sins in your body on the terrible tree, in the shadow of your cross we pray for your forgiveness. Give us such a change of heart that we may never crucify you again or bring shame to your name. Amen.

THE ASSURANCE OF PARDON:

Simon: I carried the cross to a place outside the city walls, and there they crucified the man. As he hung there in agony, he looked at the mockers who made a joke of his misery. He looked at the Jewish leaders who plotted his death. He looked at the Roman soldiers gambling for his clothes. He looked at me. He looked at the whole world, and with his dying breath he said, "Father, forgive them." *(Simon snuffs the last remaining candle, the white Christ candle.)* Can you believe it? By the word of that crucified man, you are forgiven!

EASTER— MARY MAGDALENE

(When the prelude has ended, the liturgist stands, but does not invite the congregation to stand. The liturgist says in a loud voice: "The Lord is risen!" Immediately Mary Magdalene enters the sanctuary, and joyfully responds, "He is risen indeed!" Mary is carrying the burning Christ candle that was extinguished on Good Friday.)

Mary: Have you ever had a nightmare so terrible that you couldn't bear it, as if the best thing in your life had come to an end? And then you woke up to find that the bad thing was only a dream. And you lay there in the dark with tears on your face, saying, "Thank you, God! Thank you! Thank you!"

That's how it felt when my master came to me beside the empty tomb. It was as if the worst thing in the world had turned out to be a bad dream, and the best thing in the world was standing there in front of me alive and well and smiling!

(Mary puts the Christ candle in place.)

Once Jesus was dead, but now he is alive. I have seen this with my own eyes. My Lord has come back to me, and now he will never leave me.

THE PRAYER OF ADORATION *(led by liturgist)*:

Leader: Risen Lord, Life of all who live: you have drawn us up from the grave. We cried to you for help, and you have rescued our soul from death.

People: Healer of the suffering: because of you the world is good and life is sweet. We may weep through the night, but each morning you renew our joy.

Leader: Hope of Israel and Head of the Church: you have turned our grief into dancing. You have taken away our funeral clothes and dressed us in gladness.

People: First-born from the dead, our Beginning and our End: we can't keep quiet. We will celebrate your victory. We will praise you with songs. We will give thanks to you for ever and ever! ✝

John...Mary

by Carolyn McDowell

Mary, the Mother...John, the beloved disciple: Each stands as if at the foot of the cross, facing the rear of the sanctuary as though the cross is located there. If there is a cross erected in the sanctuary, they will take their positions appropriately, making sure they can be heard distinctly. There should be enough distance between them that they seem separated. Though Jesus still lives, for them he is already gone. They are lost in their own thoughts and memories, hardly aware that the other is near. The parallel/similar phrases in each monologue should be strong.

JOHN
He is my friend.
I shall miss him.
Three years seem too short a time for love to grow so large.
And yet, my love for him has the depth and breadth of a lifetime...
a lifetime of <u>knowing,</u>
a lifetime of sharing,
a lifetime of caring for each other.
He was my friend.
I shall miss him.

MARY
He is my son.
I shall miss him.
33 years of "knowing" him, and yet I knew him not.
There was too much to know.
But does any mother ever truly know her child?
No, I think not.
There is always a stranger inside
...emerging unexpectedly in a word,
in a gesture,
in a look that is different from any seen before...
somehow always a stranger...
Still, he is my son.
I shall miss him.

JOHN
From the moment I first saw him,
I knew I had discovered my destiny.
Could I name that destiny?
No...but it needed no name. None but his.
It was enough to hear him speak,
to hear in his words, ideas— so new, so radical...yet so right.
To see in his eyes a depth of love surpassing anything of this earth...
a love that encompassed everyone, binding us in a caring oneness.
Yes, from the moment I saw him,
I knew.

MARY
From the moment I first saw him...newborn, helpless...
I knew I was part of a moment larger than life.
But what mother doesn't feel that way?
Every birth brings with it wonder and mystery.
Could this tiny babe truly be different from all others?
How?
He looked the same as other newborns.
Of course **my** child was the most beautiful ever born...
wasn't **yours**?
Yet...how would he be truly different?
From the moment I saw him I realized...
I didn't know.

JOHN
I wish you could have been with us
as we walked the length and breadth of this land:
crowds following everywhere...
miracle upon miracle...
astounding <u>us</u> no less than the blind who saw for the first time
or the lame, free at last to leap for joy.
But in a way, we had all been blind
and crippled...
blinded by old ideas,
crippled by ineffective ways of doing things.
Now we saw for the first time...
truly **saw** the world
as it was CREATED to be.

MARY
I wish you could have seen him growing into manhood.
Each day the miracle became more and more evident...
the miracle of who he really was!
But in my joy I was blinded to the danger this truth might hold for him.
I saw the world

only as I dreamed it could be...
felt it WOULD be.

JOHN
I cannot comprehend this moment.
All that is good and beautiful was manifest in this one man.
And now he hangs dying on a cross...
NO!!!!
I cannot gaze into his tortured eyes.
I, one of his trusted, chosen followers
can <u>do</u> nothing, can <u>give</u> nothing
to ease his pain.
My hands are EMPTY!

MARY
I cannot comprehend this moment.
Can so much good disappear into the oblivion of death?
Day after day I cared for him, met his every need,
fulfilled my God-ordained destiny.
And now at the point of his greatest need
I am empty... my hands are EMPTY!
Am I to do nothing?
Give nothing?

VOICE OF JESUS
(voice should be over unseen sound system)
Woman, behold your son.
Son, behold your mother.

MARY
(gazes for a few moments into the "face" of Jesus, then turns...)
John?

JOHN
(has fixed his gaze on Jesus' face...at the sound of Mary's voice, turns to look at her, then...)
Mother?
(they reach out tentatively to each other)

VOICE
Minister to each other
as you would minister unto me.
This is the truth of my life.
This is the message of my death.
Move now into a world filled with need.
Love **each other** as I have loved you.
From this moment on...
YOU BECOME MY LIFE IN THIS WORLD.

John and Mary pause for a moment, taking this all in. Then with a look of resolution in their faces and gazing toward the cross, they exit the sanctuary filled more with hope than pain. ✝

Palm Sunday
From Palm Branches to Easter Lilies

by Susan Gregg-Schroeder

Scripture: Mark 11:1-11

How we love a parade!
We line the street
And fill the sanctuaries
    to witness the triumphant entrance
    of Jesus into the city...
into our lives.

How we love the victory!
With flowers, baskets,
And things brand new,
    we come together to celebrate
    the victory of Jesus on the cross.

We move comfortably
    from Palm Sunday to Easter Sunday.
In doing so, we pass over
    the Thursdays and Fridays
    of our lives.

For God is God in suffering and death,
    just as God is God
    in blessing and life.

To reclaim Maundy Thursday
    and Good Friday
is to recognize God's presence
    in our defeats
    seeking to transform those defeats
    into new life and new possibilities. ✝

Liturgy Of The Passion

by Gwen Drake

Call to Worship

Men: Cry out, people of faith! Rejoice and praise God!

Women: If we did not sing praise, the very stones would cry out!

Men: Cry out, people of faith! For your savior draws near to Jerusalem.

Women: Hosanna! God saves! Blessed is the One who comes in God's name!

Men: Blessed is Jesus Christ, who did not turn back for fear of the cross. Let us praise the God who loves us, sharing Christ's sufferings, and facing with courage our path of faith.

Women: Hosanna! God saves! Blessed is the One who comes in God's name![1]

Hymn: "Hosanna, Loud Hosanna" *(Between verses 2 & 3, read Luke 19:29-40.)*

Introduction

The excitement of Jesus' entry into Jerusalem was short-lived and the joy was bittersweet as the events of the next few days unfolded. The story's mood changed to sadness and deep loneliness as Jesus faced the ultimate cost of being faithful to God's call.

Today's reading from the Hebrew Scriptures is from an earlier time and situation, but the early church recognized in these words from Isaiah a description of Jesus as he faced the suffering of his last hours.

Read Isaiah 50:4-9a.

Hymn: "Were You There?" Verse 1

Read Luke 19:45-46.

Dramatic Reading: An Outraged Priest
  Object: A broken piece of furniture

Did you hear about what that man Jesus did? Look at this! It's broken! But that's nothing. You should see the temple courtyard. It's a mess. All because of him! He just marched in, grabbed the money-changers' tables and pushed them over. Money went rolling everywhere. People scrambled. The animals were frightened and they scattered everywhere trying to get away. We had to close down the cleansing rituals for the day—no one could get their money changed to buy their animals.

Doesn't Jesus know what he's doing? He's confusing the people! The Romans think he's crazy! And I think he's trying to break the law and the covenant. We've got to do something to stop him. He's gone too far. This is it. I won't tolerate such disrespect and heresy anymore. It's time to do something. We need to put a stop to this, before all of us are destroyed. He has to be stopped! (Lay broken furniture in front of altar.)

Hymn: "Were You There?" Verse 2

Read Luke 22:7-23.

Dramatic Reading: A Serving Woman
  Object: Tray with empty chalice and broken bread

That was the strangest Passover meal I have ever served. I've never seen anything like it before. Oh, at the beginning it was just like every Passover meal I served at. Everything was there. The prayers were spoken. Then Jesus kept interrupting the ritual with his own words. He talked about suffering, he said something about not eating again until the Passover was fulfilled in the Kingdom of God. I thought he was talking in some kind of code language. I thought, he must know something I don't. I wondered what it was. Then I realized that the disciples didn't know either. He broke the bread and said (I'll never forget his words as long as I live), "This is my body, which is given for you. Do this in remembrance of me." And I wondered if he was leaving, going somewhere far away. It was like he wanted them to remember him. But more than that, he really wanted them to remember this particular night, this particular Passover meal.

Then he did almost the same thing with the cup. I remember exactly what he said, "This cup that is poured out for you is the new covenant in my blood."

And then it was like a shadow covered the room, making it even darker than it was. Jesus talked about one of them betraying him. The disciples got really upset. They all started talking at once, asking each other who, who could do such a thing. That didn't get anywhere so they changed the subject and started arguing about who was going to be the greatest. And then Jesus really got serious—and starting talking in riddles. He said the greatest ones are the youngest and leaders are servants. Then he told not only about a betrayer, but he said Peter was going to deny knowing him three times. Not once, but three times. Peter didn't like that one bit—he denied it. He said, "I'll go with you anywhere—even to prison!—I'll even die with you." But Jesus just sighed and went on talking with them in that gentle teaching voice that I have heard so often as I got ready to clean up. When they left, Jesus seemed really sad and tired and, well, lonely—maybe he was discouraged, I don't know. He said he was going to the garden to pray. As soon as he left, the one named Judas took off really fast. The other disciples followed Jesus to the garden. (Lay chalice and broken pieces of bread on altar.)

Hymn: "Were You There?" Verse 3

Read Luke 22:47-53

Dramatic Reading: The High Priest's Slave
Object: A bandage

I still can't believe what just happened! I can't believe it! It was a tragedy and a miracle at the same time. I can't believe it. Maybe I'll wake up and find it was all a dream. I don't know. You see, my master, the High Priest, ordered me to go to the garden. I went, of course. It was a very strange night, I had a different kind of feeling about it from the very beginning. When we got there, I saw Jesus. Then I knew something awful was going to happen. My master was very afraid of Jesus. He was so afraid that I knew he was going to do something terrible, something he probably would regret. You see, I know from experience that power and fear don't mix well together. All slaves know that only too well. I knew slaves who were killed by their masters, simply because their masters were afraid of them.

I don't know why my master was afraid of Jesus. Maybe it was because Jesus was so popular, so wise, so...I don't know. I do know that when I heard him speak I felt important, worthy, ummm...well, loved in a way I had never been loved before...maybe the word I'm looking for is...ummm...honored. Jesus didn't make me feel like a slave.

Anyway, when I saw Jesus in the garden, I knew he was in trouble. I saw Judas, one of his own disciples kiss him. But it wasn't the usual, customary kiss. There was something...well, evil about it. Then we all surrounded Jesus. My master said, "Get him. Get him." I had to obey my master. I always did. That's how I survived—following orders.

Then someone said, "Strike! Sword!" And I felt this incredible pain on the side of my head. I put my hand up there and my ear was gone. That person with the sword had cut off my ear! But then Jesus said, "No more of this!" And he touched the side of my head and healed my ear completely. You see, it was a miracle, a miracle. I just stood there, I couldn't do anything. I couldn't say anything. I just stood there and watched them take Jesus away. They took him away. And I don't know what to do. I don't know how to save him. I wish that I could save him from the fear and the power of my master. (Lay bandage on altar.)

Hymn: "Were You There?" Verse 4

Read Luke 23: 13-25.

Dramatic Reading: Woman from crowd at Pilate's court
Object: Sandal

Oh no, what have I done? What did I say? They are taking him away. Jesus. Jesus. One minute I was shouting, "Crucify him" with everyone else. What was I thinking? What was I doing? How could I have been part of this terrible thing? And now he is going away to die a death he doesn't deserve. Now they are going to crucify him. What am I going to do?

The sandal. I have his sandal. I need to get to Jesus. He lost it along the way. He needs it. But those soldiers, how can I get through the soldiers? If only I could do something, this little thing for Jesus, maybe I would feel better. Maybe then he would know that I was sorry, that I didn't mean to say those words. It all happened so fast. The crowd was so excited. I was afraid, I was excited, I got carried away. It got out of hand. We went too far. We couldn't stop. We couldn't take back the words. It was as if something was controlling us. Something dark and evil.

What am I going to do now? I can't give Jesus his sandal. It's too dangerous. I better stay back. I must be careful. (Lay the sandal on the altar.)

(Continued on page 34)

Shrove Tuesday Traditions

by Ann Bateman

Shrove Tuesday is the Tuesday immediately before Ash Wednesday. The name comes from the word "to shrive," which means to confess one's sins and receive absolution. This was a requirement before the beginning of Lent in the early Catholic Church. The church bell used to summons townspeople to church for repentance on Shrove Tuesday was called the "Shriving Bell."

Shrovetide is a term used to describe the three days preceding Ash Wednesday when the people partied and ate all the food that was forbidden during Lent. This is a traditional time for carnivals.

Another name for Shrove Tuesday is Mardi Gras, which is French for "Fat Tuesday". The name comes from the practice of trying to eat all the fatty foods in the house prior to the beginning of Lent. Two famous celebrations of Mardi Gras are held in New Orleans and Rio de Janeiro.

The traditional foods eaten for Shrove Tuesday are pancakes and doughnuts. The pancakes include all the ingredients (fats, eggs and milk) that are not used during Lent. Doughnuts—a German and Pennsylvania Dutch custom where Shrove Tuesday is called Fastnacht Eve—are considered a good luck food. Failing to eat the doughnuts could cause boils, chickens that wouldn't lay eggs, and other forms of bad luck.

A contest traditionally held on Shrove Tuesday is the Pancake Race. It began in England when a housewife heard the shriving bell ring and raced off to church with a pancake griddle still in her hand. This became an annual race between the women of the town. The first woman to the church received the vicar's blessing. Another famous pancake race is held between the towns of Olney, England and Liberal, Kansas. An open telephone line between the two towns allows the winner to be decided.

The Germans eat pretzels for Shrove Tuesday. Pretzels are made from only flour, water and salt. They were eaten instead of bread, since eggs, milk and fats were not allowed. Pretzels are twisted into the shape of two arms crossed in the act of prayer. The German name pretzel is from a Latin word meaning "little arms."

A French tradition is to make a Lenten calendar that looks like a little nun. On Ash Wednesday families draw and cut out a figure of a nun with seven feet, one for each of the weeks of Lent. As each week passes, one foot is folded back under the nun's habit. The drawing of the nun does not have a mouth, as a reminder that Lent is a time of fasting.

Shrove Tuesday Program

This final day of fun before Lent begins with frivolity and ends with a quiet time of self-evaluation often experienced in an Ash Wednesday service. It provides an opportunity for learning, fun and worship all in one evening for those caught in the unrelenting demands of work, home and school. It meets the needs of those who find it difficult to carve out two nights in one week for a special event at the church.

SUPPER: 6:00-6:30 p.m.

Serve a meal of pancakes, ham, juice and milk prepared by a group in the church, augmented by applesauce and favorite pancake toppings brought by participants. A small donation from each person will ease expenses and give a boost to some specific church project.

LEARNING: 6:00-6:40 p.m.

Placemats on the tables can provide an opportunity for learning about the various names for the day. You may also include interesting traditions about pancake races in England and the United States, mask-making and parades in New Orleans and Rio de Janiero, doughnuts as a good luck food, as well as information about Lent, its meaning and traditions. In the center of the placemat is the symbol of the seven-footed nun. The nun may be cut out and serve as a Lenten calendar. One foot is turned under on each Sunday of Lent. Following the meal an informal trivia quiz with simple questions such as, "What are two other names used for Shrove Tuesday?" and "What town in England holds a pancake race?" will test whether folks have been reading their placemats. No prizes, just lots of fun while watching people scramble to read and find the answer before someone else does.

FUN: 6:40-7:30 p.m.

Pancake Races
Mark a course on the floor of the fellowship hall with masking tape. It can be straight or winding around the room. Give participants a frying pan with a pancake. The goal is to have the fastest time over the course. Three large Xs along the course indicate where the runner must successfully flip the pancake on his or her pan. A timer with stopwatch scores each participant. Generally all the children will want to participate, youth can be encouraged to, and with some persuasion, the youth counselors, pastor, lay leader and a few other young-at-heart adults will run the course.

Pancake Toss
Ask the cooks in the kitchen to cook a few tough pancakes. These are used for the pancake toss. Create several boxes of different sizes by using masking tape on the floor; give 25 points for tossing a pancake in the smallest one, 15 for the next larger, and 10 for the largest.

Pretzel Making
Form pretzels from frozen bread dough which has been properly thawed. Sprinkle with coarse salt and bake. Talk about the tradition of Lenten pretzels and their special shape which reminds us of arms folded in prayer.

Other Activities
Mask-making, doughnut decorating, creation of Lenten calendars, and other Lenten craft and learning activities may be included as time, space, and numbers of persons warrant.

WORSHIP: 7:30-8:00 p.m.

Following the informal games and activities, invite persons to gather for instructions about the remainder of the evening: "We will all move quietly to _____ . You will hear soft music playing. Please do not talk. When you get there you may sit on the chairs or on the floor."

Plan for worship to be in a room with a fireplace, if possible. If not, a room large enough to allow for the safe burning of ashes in a large bowl may be used.

- Light candles.
- Share briefly about the season of Lent, with special emphasis on preparation, confession and sacrifice.
- Read scripture (e.g., Matthew 6:16-18).
- Invite participants to confession. Distribute paper, providing crayons for young children and pencils for others. Invite each to write or draw a prayer of confession. Suggest young children draw a picture of something they would like to say to God.
- Collect folded prayers and place them individually in the fireplace or a large fire-safe bowl (which has an air passage underneath), where they are burned.
- Sing "Jesu, Jesu" and "Kum Ba Yah".
- Anoint persons with cooled ashes as they come forward and kneel individually.
- Depart in silence. ✞

Purim----Reading Of Esther

by Christie L. Jenkins

The Jewish holiday of Purim, based on the story in the book of Esther, is celebrated each spring on the 14th of Adar (Mar/Apr) during the Christian Lenten period. (The 13th of Adar is observed as a day of fasting—the fast of Esther.) Purim celebrates the deliverance of the Jewish people by the actions of Esther and her uncle, Mordecai, from the wrath of Haman, who plotted their annihilation.

During Jesus' time this holiday was observed with a reading of the scroll of Esther, both in the temple in Jerusalem and by the people in their synagogues and homes (Mishnah Megillah). It was also customary to visit relatives and friends and to give gifts to the poor (Esther 9:22).

These early customs were retained and still are part of the modern day Jewish celebration of Purim. Over the centuries Purim has also taken on a carnival atmosphere with the eating of sweets, children dressing up in costumes, plays and parodies of the Esther story being performed, and adults drinking on this one day with abandon.

While most Christians do not celebrate Purim, some of the themes conveyed in the book of Esther have relevance as Lenten themes. Lent is a time to reflect on our relationships with other people—the story of Esther is a story of the evil that is possible when those relationships go awry. It is also a story of redemption—another Lenten/Easter theme—for through the efforts of Esther and her uncle, Mordecai, the Jewish people were spared.

Persecuted people are still very much with us and in need of assistance in order to survive. The indigenous people of the world are in danger, some threatened with extinction, and yet we often hear very little about them. There are an estimated 200-250 million indigenous people in the world and each year some 200,000 of them die. They and their cultures are threatened with extinction for various reasons—political persecution, warfare, malnutrition, disease, the young abandoning traditional ways, and deforestation.

A number of indigenous people live in the rainforest areas of the world and the best way to protect them is to protect the rainforests—their homes—from destruction. For instance, the Awara of Brazil face total extinction as loggers move into new regions, intent on destroying the mahogany forest that is the Arawa homeland.

Indigenous people for the most part know how to live in the world without causing the environmental destruction often seen in other cultures. We need their knowledge and wisdom. They have much to teach us about the wonders of God's creation. They can also remind us of our vocation to care for and preserve the earth (Gen 1:26-28; 2:15). Lent should also be a time when we examine our relationship with the environment—God's creation.

It is with these considerations in mind that the following service is presented.

A Purim Service

Processional

Hymn

Invocation

Introduction/Prayer

Choir Anthem
   Pick a selection from G.F. Handel's <u>Esther</u> or <u>Haman and Mordecai</u>

Reading From Esther
Read Esther 3:1-4:3.

Homily

- Briefly summarize the story of Esther:

  - Good triumphs over evil, life over death;
  - The outcome is determined in this case by human action, not some miraculous divine intervention;
  - Persecution results from seeing others as different, or as a threat, or as somehow less human—not as equal children of the Creator;
  - Persecution is still occurring in many parts of the world;
  - Christians must always act against persecution and genocide.
  - Discuss the plight/persecution of indigenous people—they too can teach us about our Christian vocation.

Offertory

On Purim it is the custom to collect money in remembrance of the half shekel collected from every adult male for the temple tax (Exod. 30:11-16; Matt. 17:24-27). The money is given to the poor. In keeping with this tradition, let us each put in an extra fifty cents, as we share the gifts God has given us. (Send the offering to Cultural Survival, Inc., 46 Brattle St., Cambridge, MA 02138, 617-441-5400 or Oxfam America.)

Choir/Celebrant
Psalm 133

Litany
(Consulting the references with color photographs of indigenous people given at the right, recruit someone who can make slides of some of the pictures. Project the slides during the chanting of the following litany.)

C: Save, O Lord, the _____* from those who seek to destroy them.
R: Grant this, O Lord.

C: Protect, O Lord, the _____ from persecution and ill treatment.
R: Grant this, O Lord.

C: Preserve, O Lord, the natural homes of the _____.
R: Grant this, O Lord.

C: Strengthen, O Lord, the _____ to withstand and overcome the assaults made against them.
R: Grant this, O Lord.

Masai (Kenya), Penan (Malaysia), Chukchi (Russia), Ainu (Japan), Shimako (Peru), Yanomami (Brazil), Lacandon (Chiapas, Mexico), Igarot (Phillipines), Arawa (Brazil), Amuesha (Peru), Cubeo (Ecuador), San (Africa), Sherpas (Nepal), etc.

Concluding Prayer

God, You have made us all one family, truly cousins in the flesh and brothers and sisters in the Spirit. Forgive us when we forget this and act either deliberately or ignorantly in ways that cause harm. Help us to act in ways that will be a blessing to the whole human family.

The Lord's Prayer

Benediction
Psalm 67

Hymn

Recessional

The coffee hour can reflect some of the joyous aspects of the Purim holiday. Hold a Rainforest Bake Sale. Make some sweets or desserts using some ingredients from rainforest plants (chocolate, allspice, avocado, rice, vanilla, brazil nuts, cashews, oranges, bananas, etc.). Send the proceeds to Cultural Survival, Inc. or some organization working to preserve the world's rainforests. ✞

References:

Burger, J. The Gaia Atlas of First Peoples: A Future for the Indigenous World. Gaia/Anchor, 1990.

Cultural Survival. State of the Peoples: A Global Human Rights Report on Peoples in Danger. Boston: Beacon Press, 1993.

Davidson, A., Endangered Peoples. Sierra Club Books, 1993.

Genno, A. ed. Amazonia: Voices from the Rainforest—A Resource and Action Guide. San Francisco: Rainforest Action Network, 1990.

Liddell, M.A. "Twilight of the Tribes?" Smithsonian (Nov. 1993), 78-85.

Linden, E. "Lost Tribes, Lost Knowledge," Time (Sept. 23, 1991), 46-56.

The Darkening Service

by Denise Krebs

"Tenebrae" is the Latin term for "darkness," a literal and figurative description of what happened to the world when Christ died on the cross. A service of tenebrae and holy communion is celebrated on Maundy Thursday or Good Friday. This service is a significant and penetrating way to present the story of the Last Supper, the arrest, trial, crucifixion, death, and burial of Jesus. Individuals and groups from the congregation are recruited to read the parts of Peter, Jesus, Judas, Pilate, the religious leaders, and other biblical players. A most meaningful and humbling part of the service is when the liturgy directs the entire congregation to shout, "Let him be crucified!" A sample tenebrae service employing the Gospel of Matthew, in the New Revised Standard Version, is presented below. This service has been developed over the years by Rev. Marlin VanderWilt, pastor of the Church of the Cross, Sarasota, Florida, Reformed Church in America. He reworks the service each year using the Synoptic gospel reading in the common lectionary for Lent and Easter.

Throughout the service, the readings are supported with hymns, choral anthems, a meditation and holy communion. Candelabras, with candles, and house lighting, are used to darken the room gradually after each reading. At the end of the service, the only lighting in the church is the Christ candle held in the center of a large, rough, wooden cross. The congregation is dismissed in silence and darkness, except for the Christ candle, representing Jesus, the eternal light in a dark world. This emotional and solemn ending is a fitting way to leave the church, anticipating the celebration of Easter. On Easter morning, the same cross is turned around to reveal a finished white cross, with cubicles to hold potted Easter lilies in celebration of the resurrection.

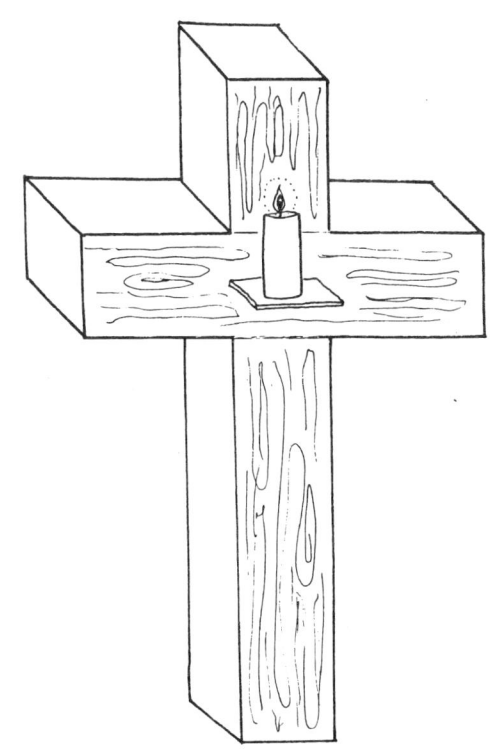

(Five-foot tall, three-dimensional cross, made with rough, unfinished wood. There is a small shelf to hold the Christ candle.)

A Service of Tenebrae and Holy Communion

As the passion story unfolds in scripture, the power of darkness increases until only one light remains—the Christ candle, the light of God's love and promise to be faithful. Our passion narrative this year is from the Gospel of Matthew.

PRELUDE

VOTUM

SALUTATION

HYMN: "In the Cross of Christ I Glory"

PRAYER OF CONFESSION (*responsively*):

Pastor: Why is this night special? Why on this night do we break bread and drink from this cup?

People: This night is important for all Christians because, at this time, Jesus celebrated the Passover with his disciples for the last time. He broke the bread and said it was his body. He poured the cup and said it was his blood poured out for the forgiveness of sins.

Pastor: What do we do when we celebrate the Last Supper?

People: We remember the death of Jesus who died for us; we celebrate his presence with us tonight; and we pray that he will come again to make all things right.

Pastor: Let us then pray in silence, seeking his forgiveness for past sins; his power to make the present full of purpose; and his help for future hope.

People: We bow in silence before his cross.

ASSURANCE OF PARDON

READING I—THE PREPARATION FOR COMMUNION

Narrator: On the first day of unleavened bread the disciples came to Jesus, saying,

Disciple: "Where do you want us to make the preparations for you to eat the Passover?"

Jesus: "Go into the city to a certain man and say to him, 'The Teacher says, My time is near; I will keep the Passover at your house with my disciples.'"

Narrator: So the disciples did as Jesus had directed them, and they prepared the Passover meal.

SCRIPTURE READING

MEDITATION

HYMN: "Beneath the Cross of Jesus"

THE LAST SUPPER
    Prayer of Consecration
    The Invitation

READING II—THE BREAD AND THE CUP

Narrator: While they were eating, Jesus took a loaf of bread, and after blessing it he broke it, gave it to the disciples, and said,

Jesus: "Take, eat; this is my body."

Narrator: Then he took a cup, and after giving thanks, he gave it to them, saying,

Jesus: "Drink from it, all of you; for this is my blood of the covenant, which is poured out for many for the forgiveness of sins. I tell you, I will never again drink of this fruit of the vine until that day when I drink it new with you in my Father's kingdom."

COMMUNION: "You are invited to come forward to the table placed before you. Please begin with the front pews, coming one row at a time."

HYMN: "O Sacred Head Now Wounded"

READING III—THE ARREST

Narrator: When they had sung the hymn, they went out to the Mount of Olives. Then Jesus said to them,

Jesus: "You will all become deserters because of me this night; for it is written, 'I will strike the shepherd, and the sheep of the flock will be scattered.' But after I am raised up, I will go ahead of you to Galilee."

Narrator: Peter said to him,

Peter: "Though all become deserters because of you, I will never desert you."

Jesus: "Truly I tell you, this very night, before the cock crows, you will deny me three times."

Peter: "Even though I must die with you, I will not deny you."

Narrator: And so said all the disciples. Then Jesus went with them to a place called Gethsemane; and he said to his disciples,

Jesus: "Sit here while I go over there and pray."

Narrator: He took with him Peter and the two sons of Zebedee, and began to be grieved and agitated. Then he said to them,

Jesus: "I am deeply grieved, even to death; remain here, and stay awake with me."

Narrator: And going a little farther, he threw himself on the ground and prayed,

Jesus: "My Father, if it is possible, let this cup pass from me; yet not what I want but what you want."

Narrator: Then he came to the disciples and found them sleeping; and he said to Peter,

Jesus: "So, could you not stay awake with me one hour? Stay awake and pray that you may not come into the time of trial; the spirit indeed is willing, but the flesh is weak."

Narrator: Again he went away for the second time and prayed,

Jesus: "My Father, if this cannot pass unless I drink it, your will be done."

Narrator: Again he came and found them sleeping, for their eyes were heavy. So, leaving them again, he went away and prayed for the third time, saying the same words. Then he came to the disciples and said to them,

Jesus: "Are you still sleeping and taking your rest? See, the hour is at hand, and the son of Man is betrayed into the hands of sinners. Get up, let us be going. See, my betrayer is at hand."

Narrator: While he was still speaking, Judas, one of the twelve, arrived; with him was a large crowd with swords and clubs, from the chief priests and the elders of the people. Now the betrayer had given them a sign, saying,

Judas: "The one I will kiss is the man; arrest him."

Narrator: At once he came up to Jesus and said,

Judas: "Greetings, Rabbi!"

Narrator: and kissed him. Jesus said to him,

Jesus: "Friend, do what you are here to do."

Narrator: Then they came and laid hands on Jesus and arrested him.

CHORAL ANTHEM

PRAYER OF INTERCESSION

READING IV—THE TRIAL BEFORE PILATE

Narrator: When morning came, all the chief priests and the elders of the people conferred together against Jesus in order to bring about his death. They bound him, led him away, and handed him over to Pilate the governor. Now Jesus stood before the governor, and the governor asked him,

Pilate: "Are you the King of the Jews?"

Jesus: "You say so."

Narrator: But when he was accused by the chief priests and elders, he did not answer. Then Pilate said to him,

Pilate: "Do you not hear how many accusations they make against you?"

Narrator: But he gave him no answer, not even to a single charge, so that the governor was greatly amazed. Now, at the festival, the governor was accustomed to release a prisoner for the crowd, anyone whom they wanted. At that time they had a notorious prisoner, called Jesus Barabbas. So after they had gathered, Pilate said to them,

Pilate: "Whom do you want me to release for you, Jesus Barabbas or Jesus who is called the Messiah?"

Narrator: For he realized that it was out of jealousy that they had handed him over. While he was sitting on the judgment seat, his wife sent word to him,

Pilate's Wife: "Have nothing to do with that innocent man, for today I have suffered a great deal because of a dream about him."

Narrator: Now the chief priests and the elders persuaded the crowds to ask for Barabbas and to have Jesus killed. The governor again said to them,

Pilate: "Which of the two do you want me to release for you?"

People: "Barabbas."

Pilate: "Then what should I do with Jesus who is called the Messiah?"

Narrator: All of them said,

People: "Let him be crucified!"

Pilate: "Why, what evil has he done?"

Narrator: But they shouted all the more,

People: "Let him be crucified!"

Narrator: So when Pilate saw that he could do nothing, but rather that a riot was beginning, he took some water and washed his hands before the crowd, saying,

Pilate: "I am innocent of this man's blood; see to it yourselves."

Narrator: Then the people as a whole answered,

People: "His blood be on us and on our children!"

Narrator: So he released Barabbas for them; and after flogging Jesus, he handed him over to be crucified.

HYMN: "Ah, Holy Jesus How Hast Thou Offended"

READING V—THE CRUCIFIXION

Narrator: Then the soldiers of the governor took Jesus into the governor's headquarters, and they gathered the whole cohort around him. They stripped him and put a scarlet robe on him, and after twisting some thorns into a crown, they put it on his head. They put a reed in his right hand and knelt before him and mocked him, saying,

People: "Hail, King of the Jews!"

Narrator: They spat on him, and took the reed and struck him on the head. After mocking him, they stripped him of the robe and put his own clothes on him. Then they led him away to crucify him. As they went out, they came upon a man from Cyrene named Simon; they compelled this man to carry his cross. And when they came to a place called Golgotha (which means Place of a Skull), they offered him wine to drink, mixed with gall; but when he tasted it, he would not drink it. And when they had crucified him, they divided his clothes among themselves by casting lots; then they sat down there and kept watch over him. Over his head they put the charge against him, which read, "This is Jesus, the King of the Jews." Then two bandits were crucified with him, one on his right and one on his left. Those who passed by derided him, shaking their heads and saying,

People: "You who would destroy the temple and build it in three days, save yourself! If you are the son of God, come down from the cross."

Narrator: In the same way the chief priests also, along with the scribes and elders, were mocking him, saying,

Religious Leaders: "He saved others; he cannot save himself. He is the King of Israel; let him come down from the cross now, and we will believe in him. He trusts in God; let God deliver him now, if he wants to; for he said, 'I am God's son.'"

Narrator: The bandits who were crucified with him also taunted him in the same way. From noon on, darkness came over the whole land until three in the afternoon. At about three o'clock Jesus cried with a loud voice,

Jesus: "Eli, Eli, lema sabachthani? My God, my God, why have you forsaken me?"

CHORAL ANTHEM

READING VI—THE DEATH OF JESUS

Narrator: Then Jesus cried again with a loud voice and breathed his last. At that moment the curtain of the temple was torn in two, from top to bottom. The earth shook, and the rocks were split. The tombs also were opened, and many bodies of the saints who had fallen asleep were raised. After his resurrection they came out of the tombs and entered the holy city and appeared to many. Now when the centurion and those with him, who were keeping watch over Jesus, saw the earthquake and what took place, they were terrified and said,

People: "Truly this man was God's son!"

HYMN: "Were You There?" *(verses 1-3)*

READING VII—THE BURIAL OF JESUS

Narrator: Many women were also there, looking on from a distance; they had followed Jesus from Galilee and had provided for him. Among them were Mary Magdalene, and Mary the mother of James and Joseph, and Mary the mother of the sons of Zebedee. When it was evening, there came a rich man from Arimathea, named Joseph, who was also a disciple of Jesus. He went to Pilate and asked for the body of Jesus; then Pilate ordered it to be given to him. So Joseph took the body and wrapped it in a clean linen cloth and laid it in his own new tomb, which he had hewn in the rock. He then rolled a great stone to the door of the tomb and went away. Mary Magdalene and the other Marys were there, sitting opposite the tomb.

DISMISSAL: Depart in darkness and silence. ✛

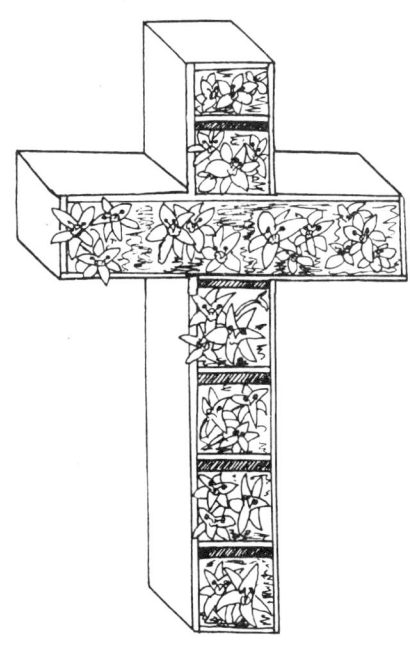

This side of the cross is smooth and painted white. There are open, downward-tilting shelves to hold potted Easter lilies.

Quotations from the Bible are taken from the New Revised Standard Version, copyright ©1989 by the Division of Christian Education of the National Council of the Churches of Christ in the United States of America.

Tenebrae Journey...
Past And Present

by Carolyn McDowell

TECHNICAL INFORMATION

This drama was designed to follow a communion service. During the serving of the elements, the choir sang "One Bread, One Body," #620 from the 1989 edition of the <u>United Methodist Hymnal</u>. The last 2 braces/scores of this hymn are the musical setting for the refrains sung by the choir to punctuate each of the drama scenes.

The Speech Choir and Singing Choir were the same group of 4 people. The number of people involved is optional. Our group was placed in the rear balcony so there was less distraction at the front where the action took place.

The character of Tenebrae enters after the communion service. He/she is clothed completely in black (we used a choir robe) and the head is covered with a sheer black veil allowing the features to be seen, but dimly. Tenebrae remains the center throughout the scene, standing behind a small table upon which is placed the large Christ Candle which has been lit earlier by an acolyte. At the end, it is this candle which is carried into the darkness. On either side of the front area are candelabra and two acolytes. As the service progresses, candles are gradually extinguished so that at the end only the Christ Candle is glowing. Since the playing area might become too dark for the characters to be seen, general house lights should be available and gradually lowered as the candles are extinguised, leaving enough light for the last drama scene. As Tenebrae exits, all house lighting should fade away so the candle itself is the only light visible.

Storm In Final Scene: In our church we erect a tall wooden cross in the front loft area and drape the cross beam with fabric strips in various shades of purple. Red spotlights are concealed at the base of the cross, focused to provide the best reflection of red on the cross and on area walls. These are controlled by a flasher unit. We have a Casio 5000 synthesizer which has an incredible wind sound on D8 preset. Low clusters of organ pedals played on the darkest tonal stop will provide a thunder effect. The "storm" is sustained for around 15-20 seconds then dies down gradually, leaving just the red glow on the cross. House lights are raised only enough for safe exit.

TENEBRAE ENTERS FROM REAR OF CHURCH, MOVING SLOWLY DOWN AISLE, TO TAKE POSITION BEHIND CHRIST CANDLE TABLE.

TENEBRAE:
I am the spirit of this night...I am darkness.
My face is veiled and shadowed.
With me comes a sense of fear and uncertainty.
The mists of evening envelop my movements...
I seem suspended between heaven and earth.
This night, begun in fellowship and feasting,
Turns now to tears and temptation.
I fill the heart of Judas so that he is even now
betraying his Master and friend.
I cloud the eyes of the remaining eleven
so that sleep rises as a wall between them
and the suffering son of God.
I walk beside the soldiers and priests on their way
to the dark destiny of Gethsemane confrontation.
I AM DARKNESS.
I am the secrets of your life carefully hidden, yet known to
God.
I am the fears and uncertainties that corrode your daily
faith.
I sit with you in your pew, nudging your doubts
needling your discontents.

I cloud your eyes as you seek the truth of this night,
so that you lose any sense of personal involvement...
so that you build a wall between yourself and this
suffering son of God.

My color is black, the absence of all light...
the blackness of death without resurrection...
The bleakness of relationship without forgiveness...
The color of life without love.
Together we will plunge into the abyss of darkness.
The savior of the world is betrayed...crucified!
Travel with me...sense my spirit...
enter the shadows of...
Gethsemane.

SPEECH CHOIR: Long ago? Far away? Distant past or poignant NOW?

VOICE 1: Gethsemane...a timeless testament...

VOICE 2: A garden calling each of us to kneel...

VOICE 3: To gaze again into that Galilean darkness...

VOICE 4: To see once more the figure bent in painful prayer.

TENEBRAE:
Wrap round yourselves the shadows of this night.
Focus not merely on remembered past.
Scan also generations yet unborn.
The suffering Savior assumes far more than ancient sins.

ALL CHARACTERS EXCEPT FREEDOM FIGHTER MOVE INTO POSITIONS ON EITHER SIDE OF TENEBRAE, THEIR BACKS TO AUDIENCE. "PAST" ACTORS TO STAGE RIGHT, "PRESENT" ACTORS TO STAGE LEFT. AT THE END OF THEIR PORTION, AS THE CHOIR SINGS, THOSE ACTORS EXIT DOWN AISLE IN CHARACTER.

SPEECH CHOIR: Peter, man of rock, awake! Your time has come!

PETER: *(BIBLICAL DRESS; TURNING SWIFTLY INTO POSITION, SWORD IN HAND, PROTECTING UNSEEN JESUS)* I'm awake now and ready, Lord! Don't worry. I'll take care of this matter...stand behind me...careful now...I can hear them moving through Gethsemane. Mark, Andrew, John—hide over there behind those rocks. We'll ambush them as they round the bend in the path. Our time has come! No more bondage to the Roman invaders! Our freedom is at hand! Thy kingdom come, O Lord!

FREEDOM FIGHTER: *(GUERRILLA ATTIRE; ENTERS FROM REAR, RUNNING FORWARD DOWN AISLE, SHOUTING, STICK IN HAND—MUCH THE SAME PHYSICAL STANCE AS PETER)* *Muslims, Croats, Palestinians: our time has come. We will no longer be oppressed. Our freedom is at hand. The only language our enemies understand is force. So be it! Then let us truly speak ONE language: the language of BLOOD. The severed ears of our enemies shall be our trophies of honor. Thy kingdom come, O Lord! (*Substitute appropriate names of people/nations engaged in conflict somewhere in the world.)*

CHOIR: *(SUNG)*
Take up the sword!
Our time has come!
We will no longer wait!

TENEBRAE: And in the garden darkness, the willing son assumes the guilt of all those who, blinded by anger, take up the sword.

SPEECH CHOIR: Judas—man of impatience—speak out!

JUDAS: *(BIBLICAL DRESS; TURNS TO FACE CONGREGATION, SPEAKING TO THEM DIRECTLY)*
Three years of dust and dirt, three years of poverty...three years of talk and promises! How long was I supposed to wait? Life is too short! If you've got the power, use it! All right, so I betrayed my friends. So I went against all I had learned, all my life had stood for. So what's wrong with taking a short cut? Everybody does it. OK! So it didn't turn out the way I expected. So what am I supposed to do? Kill myself?

STOCKBROKER: *(DRESSED IN BUSINESS SUIT, BRIEFCASE; TURNS, MIMICS JUDAS' ATTITUDE, TALKING AGAIN TO AUDIENCE)* Insider trading? So what? Look, I'm a little wheel in a big machine. Who's to know? The top guys get all the breaks. I'd never make it going by the rules. And who's it going to hurt? So I make a little profit for myself, pay my bills— put something aside for a rainy day. Values? Who cares about values these days? Life's too short. Look out for Number One! Do your own thing. Don't look at me that way! What am I supposed to do? Kill myself?

CHOIR: *(SUNG)*
I cannot cope!
Life is too hard!
I'll take the easy way!

TENEBRAE:
Tears of pain blur his eyes
eyes that gaze toward future generations
seduced by quick and easy solutions.
The cross looms nearer...

SPEECH CHOIR: Caiaphas, keeper of law: speak to us!

CAIAPHAS: *(COSTUMED AS HIGH PRIEST)* What is there left to say? Messiahs were a dime a dozen in those days. A savior on every street corner. So this one was a little different. So he spoke of love and reconciliation, brought healing and peace to those he touched. So what? That isn't the point. We Hebrews have centuries of tradition and rules preserved in minute detail concerning these matters. The law is clear: no one can claim to be the son of God!

TENEBRAE: Except...the son of God.

JUDGE: *(DRESSED IN JUDICIAL ROBES)* The law is clear, he says. How I wish it were that simple. I was elected judge by campaigning on a platform of law and order—justice for both the accused and victim, strict adherance to the law of the land. I am daily surrounded by shelves of books, libraries overflowing with the minute details of trials and legal precedents. But where do I go to find rulings on love and reconciliation, on healing and peace within a rigid interpretation of law? Where?

CHOIR: *(SUNG)*
What is the law?
What is right?
Where is the truth for me?

SPEECH CHOIR:
Woman...woman...
who...are... you?

WOMAN PAST: *(BIBLICAL ATTIRE, HEAD COVERED, FURTIVE, IMMEDIATELY DEFENSIVE, TURNS)* Who wants to know? Leave me alone. I don't know anything! I'm just part of the crowd. That man they're looking for in the garden...I don't know anything about him...just saw him from a distance once or twice. What's he got to do with me anyway? Look, if you're wanting character witnesses, you've picked the wrong person. I mind my own business. I'm not about to stick my neck out and risk getting crucified. *(looks into audience, shouts:)* Stop staring at me!

SPEECH CHOIR: Woman...Woman...What say you of risk?

WOMAN PRESENT: *(MODERN DRESS; TURNS ABRUPTLY, STARTLED)* Risk? Who, me? Not on your life. I've got my can of mace, I've got timers on all my house lamps. I'm in before dark...deadbolt locks on all the doors. *(realizes she's missed the point)* Oh, wait a minute, you're not talking about that kind of risk, are you? You're talking about creative ideas, new responsibilities, new challenges. Oh, I get it now! You're accusing me of not taking a courageous stand on important issues. Well, I won't accept that blame. There are plenty of activists out there who get their kicks from constantly stirring up trouble. What I need is peace! Isn't that what Jesus came to bring? Isn't that what he died for?

CHOIR: *(SUNG)*
Don't look to me!
It's not my fault!
I cannot take the risk!

TENEBRAE: Jesus rises from his knees.

TENEBRAE PICKS UP CHRIST CANDLE AND BEGINS RECESSIONAL UP AISLE. IF WALKING AND TALKING IS TOO DIFFICULT, HAVE ACOLYTE CARRY CANDLE, WITH TENEBRAE FOLLOWING.

TENEBRAE:
The cross is still to come,
yet across his shoulders even now
drops the yoke of our bloody angers,
our selfish impatience,
our ethical failures,
our endless rationalizations...
the weighty sins of unborn generations—
unborn yet fiercely loved as only God can love.
The last dark journey is begun.

VOICE 1: Who will walk with him,

VOICE 2: Who will wipe his brow,

VOICE 3: Who will share his pain,

VOICE 4: Who will quench his thirst?

TENEBRAE: *(FROM REAR OF SANCTUARY IF RECESSION OF CANDLE IS COMPLETE)*
Who will lighten his burden by removing the weight of
your anger,
your impatience,
your rigidity,
your rationalizations?

SPEECH CHOIR: Who?

THE STORM AND LIGHTNING EFFECTS BEGIN, RISE IN INTENSITY, THEN GRADUALLY QUIET, LEAVING ONLY A RED GLOW ON THE CROSS AREA. IN THE SILENCE FOLLOWING THE STORM, THE SPEECH CHOIR SPEAKS.

SPEECH CHOIR:
Rise now, walk into the world.
Give him...your love,
give him ... your life.
Journey from darkness
to...
resurrection light.

THE CONGREGATION LEAVES IN SILENCE. THIS INSTRUCTION SHOULD BE PRINTED IN THE BULLETIN. HOUSE LIGHTS UP ENOUGH FOR SAFETY ONLY. ✝

Maundy Thursday

by Ann Bateman

Quiet Music

Call To Worship

> **One:** Let the name of the Lord be praised!
> **All: We who are servants of the Lord offer our praise.**
> **One:** Let the mighty acts of God be praised!
> **All: We who are servants of God offer our praise.**
> **One:** Let the glory of the Holy One be praised!
> **All: We who are servants of the Holy One offer our praise.**

Words Of Introduction

We come this night in a time of remembrance that Jesus was servant to his friends. He demonstrated his hospitality and his love in the simple act of washing their feet. As we think about the love we share with our friends, we will offer to wash their hands in a holy act of hospitality.

Hymn—"Jesus' Hands Were Kind Hands"[1]

Hearing The Story—John 13:2-17, 21-26

Sharing The Story

You are invited to respond to three questions with persons sitting near you. What would be equivalent in the world today to what Jesus did to Peter? Who are the "foot-washers" of society today? Where have you had your "feet washed" this past week?

Hymn—"Jesu, Jesu"[2]

Act Of Hospitality And Servanthood

The Invitation
You who name yourself Christian, come to the basin of Jesus to renew your commitment to servanthood. Come with heart and mind of hospitality as you take up the towel. Remember the words of Jesus when he said the first shall be last. Come, you who are servants.

The Washing
You are invited to come to one of the basins to have your hands washed and then to wash the hands of the person behind you. When you have completed washing the hands of another, you may choose to pray at the communion rail or return to your seat by the side aisle.

As you wash the hands of another you may say **"In obedience to Christ, I am your servant."** As your hands are washed, you may respond **"Amen"**.

Prayer Of Personal Commitment *(unison)*

We come, O God, with renewed gratitude for Christ, who came to serve. Grant that we who have been washed, and washed another's hands in return, may continue to experience the cleansing of Your love. Help us to serve all in the human family with this same spirit of hospitality until Your love conquers all proud hearts and Your realm rules over all, through Jesus the Christ, our Lord. Amen.

Hymn Of Commitment—"They Will Know We Are Christians By Our Love"

(The community will gather in a circle and sing two verses of the hymn.)

Dismissal With Blessing

May the hospitality you have experienced here go with you and be felt by all whom you meet. Amen. ✝

---

[1] "Jesus' Hands Were Kind Hands", The United Methodist Hymnal, 1989, p. 273.
[2] "Jesu, Jesu", The United Methodist Hymnal, 1989, p. 432.

The Confession

by Carolyn McDowell

NARRATOR: (Matthew 26:57,69-75) And those who had seized Jesus led him away to Caiaphas, the high priest, where the scribes and the elders were gathered together. Now Peter was sitting outside in the courtyard, and a certain servant girl came to him and said, "You, too, were with Jesus, the Galilean." But he denied it before them all, saying, "I do not know what you are talking about." And when he had gone out to the gateway, another servant girl saw him and said to those who were there, "This man was with Jesus of Nazareth." And again he denied it with an oath, "I do not know the man." And a little later the bystanders came up and said to Peter, "Surely you, too, are one of them, for the way you talk gives you away." Then he began to curse and swear, "I do not know the man!" And immediately a cock crowed. Peter then remembered the words which Jesus had said, "Before a cock crows, you will deny me three times," and he went and wept bitterly.

(Peter enters from rear of Chapel, running blindly down aisle. Sobbing, he throws himself across the communion rail in grief. After a few moments we see/hear the servant girl who has followed Peter. She approaches him cautiously.)

GIRL: Sir...Sir...

PETER: What? *(recognizes her as the servant of the high priest who first approached him...struggles to his feet)* What do you want? I told you! I don't...I don't know... *(can't bring himself to deny Jesus yet another time... turns away from her)* O, God! What have I done? *(overcome with remorse)*

GIRL: Then you admit it: you DO know Jesus, the Galilean?

PETER: *(silence, then he turns slowly, determined now to in some way make amends)* Yes, I know him! YES, I was with him! YES, I am from Galilee. Yes, YES...YES! Why couldn't I say that word when you spoke to me in the high priest's courtyard? What kind of a man would deny his... *(stops, still unwilling to acknowledge Jesus)*

GIRL: Friend? Then he is only a friend, nothing more? *(hopeful, but in receiving no encouragement from Peter is disappointed)* Nothing more.

PETER: *(tuning in to her deeper question)* Who are you?

GIRL: You know...I am the kitchen maid for Caiaphas, the high priest.

PETER: *(suspiciously aggressive)* And perhaps also a spy, doing the dirty work of the Pharisees, trying to trap all of us who know and follow the Lord? *(too late he realizes he has revealed his belief)*

GIRL: Lord? You called him Lord!

PETER: *(is tempted to cover his tracks, then gives up further pretense)* Yes: "Lord," "son of God," "Messiah"..."Master"...all that and more, if there can be more. Jesus is everything! AND my friend. *(with irony)* I say that bravely now in darkness to a servant girl...here...HERE where my "confession" risks nothing. *(now seeking to rationalize and excuse himself)* But Jesus has to understand: back there I was too...too...

GIRL: *(finishes the sentence for him)* ...afraid. *(Peter reacts in humiliation, turns away from her.)* You're embarrassed. Why? Do you think you are the only one who knows the meaning of fear? Fear has walked beside me for as long as I have memory: fear of dying, fear of LIVING, fear of masters such as the not-so-pious priests, fear of God, himself, so distant and cold. I understand perfectly your instinct for self-preservation. Survival has become my only religion, my God. Yes...your fear I understand. But your remorse, no. You may have denied Jesus with words, but we all read "confession" in your guilty reaction to the crowing cock. Your identity was clear: a disciple of the prisoner, Jesus of Nazareth.

PETER: Was I that obvious? *(moves away, remembering with anguish)* You know, I don't remember a single thing after that...sound...nothing until I found myself here and heard your voice. That cursed rooster! Its crowing echoes in my head...louder and louder. *(pauses, then decides to share more deeply with the girl)* Jesus knew I would deny him.

GIRL: Knew? How could he be certain of such a thing?

PETER: He knew about Judas, also.

GIRL: Judas Iscariot, son of Simeon? The one who sold him to the chief priests? Judas was a disciple also? What kind of followers are you? Betraying, denying the very one you call the Messiah?

PETER: Followers? Oh, yes: chosen followers...all hand-picked by Jesus himself. And he knew us so very well. He saw strengths we never knew we possessed, but he saw our weakness too: our stubborn failure to understand what he was trying so hard to teach us, our petty fears, our little power plays...And yet he kept on loving us with all his heart and soul.

GIRL: *(remembering)* "Love the Lord, your God, with all your heart, and with all your soul, and with all your mind, and love your neighbor as yourself."

PETER: *(startled)* Where did you hear those words?

GIRL: Jesus said them.

PETER: I thought you didn't know him.

GIRL: It was you that denied knowing him, not me.

PETER: But where...?

GIRL: Several weeks ago, as I was shopping for fruit in the marketplace, I heard voices raised louder than the usual babble. Several were Pharisees, ones who had met secretly with Caiaphas. *(getting caught up with the drama of her narration)* I crept closer to overhear their conversation. In my job you can never tell when a valuable tidbit of gossip might come in handy. Well, there he was.

PETER: *(impatiently interrupting)* WHO?

GIRL: Jesus! Who else are we talking about? Jesus! He was right in the middle of that bunch. Some of the Sadducees were there too, asking questions, trying to trick him, I figured. But you know, he had an answer for every one of them. It was great. He shut them up, right there on the spot.

PETER: How? What did they ask? *(hungry to hear any word from Jesus' lips)* What did <u>he</u> answer?

GIRL: I don't remember much. Most of it was too complicated for me. *(Peter turns away disappointed...she follows anxious to please, to meet his obvious need)* There was lot of stuff about the law and Caesar and Abraham. You know how those people are. The Pharisees argue with the Sadducees, who argue with the Levites, who argue with the scribes and chief priests, who argue with anyone they can find. But I do remember Jesus' words about loving with all your heart and soul and mind. It was the sound of it.

PETER: What do you mean, "the sound of it?"

GIRL: There was something in his voice, in the way he said it. They weren't just empty words. He meant them. I knew <u>he</u> loved that way...he loved even those "snakes" who were trying to trap him. Then his words seemed to reach out toward me like he knew I was there listening.

PETER: Did he see you?

GIRL: No, I'm sure he didn't. At least he never looked in my direction. But I can't forget his voice and those words. It's like the sound of the crowing cock you keep hearing, his words are there all the time. I try, but I can't block them out. It's like he's calling to me. I don't know what to do. I thought maybe, you knowing him and all, that you could help me understand. It's too late now to ask him.

PETER: What do you mean "too late"? He's done nothing wrong. They can't hold him.

GIRL: You think they'll let him go? You are a fool! I've heard them plotting. They want him dead and they'll find some way to do it legally.

PETER: Legally? No! The Sanhedrin can't carry out a death sentence. They need the Romans for that.

GIRL: The Romans, you say? Well, that's where they're taking him now. Straight to Pilate himself. *(Peter reacts in agony across these next lines.)* Oh, yes! Caiaphas will find a way to use the Romans to do his dirty work if he has to bribe all of Jerusalem. They'll strike Jesus down and all his followers will be scattered like sheep.

PETER: What did you say? *(breaking out of his pain... hearing only the last phrase of her statement)*

GIRL: About the bribes? About striking Jesus down? *(can't seem to find the phrase Peter seeks)*

PETER: No...scattered...something about scattered...

GIRL: Scattered like sheep?

PETER: "Scattered like sheep". That's it! I've heard those words before, just tonight, earlier this evening! *(frustrated, pacing ...getting more and more agitated)* When was it? *(remembers)* Oh, yes...I remember now. It must have been just after the Passover meal. Jesus was saying some strange things about his body and blood and some kind of new covenant and...no...no, it must have been later, when we had reached the Garden of Gethsemane. He said, "You will all fall away because of me this night", and then he quoted the prophet, Zachariah: "I will strike down the shepherd, and the sheep of the flock shall be scattered."

GIRL: But Zachariah was talking about the coming Messiah.

PETER: I told you: Jesus IS that promised one, the son of God!

GIRL: The son of God? There's your answer. They can't kill him! God won't let them. God will do something to... *(she is excited, babbling on when Peter interrupts forcefully...)*

PETER: Hush, there's more. I'm trying to remember. He said

(Continued on page 34)

Good Friday Service Of Remembrance

by Maren Tirabassi

This one-hour Good Friday evening service moves from the church sanctuary to the church parlor to combine the scripture story of the death of Jesus of Nazareth with an opportunity to talk about the meaning of Jesus' life. This worship occasion suggests that what the disciples were doing during the emptiness of Good Friday evening was sharing in the Upper Room the stories of healings, miracles and parables, and the call by Jesus of each of them to follow him. Assuming that Mary, Jesus' mother, was among them, the stories of his birth would be told as well. In addition to profound sadness, the tone of the service is of gratitude, as it might be in "visiting hours" or at a "wake".

This service assumes only a small number out of the full congregation will attend worship on Good Friday. Forty-five participants or less is a comfortable number. This service is appropriate for a single church or for an ecumenical gathering. The congregation meets in the sanctuary for the opening portion of the service and then moves to a parlor or fellowship room with a circle of chairs. A center coffee table may contain objects which will remind people of biblical stories—a water jug, fish net, stone, loaf of bread, creche, bowl of seeds. The Invitation to Remembrance encourages people to share aloud their favorite stories about Jesus in a few sentences. People will offer their stories, a "my favorite is the story of the woman with the hemorrhage who reached out for Jesus' hem," a "mine is the stilling of the storm," or "mine is the birth in Bethlehem..." Some people will simply name the story and others will tell why it is meaningful.

At some point a member of the congregation will tell the group that his or her "favorite" story about Jesus is not from scripture, but something that happened in her or his life, and will then share that situation. When the stories which come from this activity are concluded, there are evening prayers which may be participatory, or led by someone who can draw together common themes and current concerns of the world and the congregation.

Order of Worship

PRELUDE OR SOLO

WELCOME

INVOCATION: Gracious God, we gather this evening to remember with love and tears the life, suffering and death of Jesus of Nazareth. We believe that this rejected man of sorrows has borne our griefs and been wounded for our transgressions. We come to this worship in deep repentance for our individual sins and in recommitment of our lives to end suffering, pain and death in all times and places. Amen.

HYMN: "Were You There When They Crucified My Lord?"

SCRIPTURE READING: Mark 15

ORGAN MEDITATION: "I Love to Tell the Story"

HYMN: "Jesus Walked This Lonesome Valley" (Sing two verses in the sanctuary, then go to the parlor and sing the third verse.)

INVITATION TO REMEMBRANCE

HYMN: "I Wonder as I Wander Out Under the Sky"

TIME TOR TELLING STORIES

HYMN: "I Love to Tell the Story"

EVENING PRAYERS, PRAYERS OF THE PEOPLE

UNISON PRAYER:
O God of all people,
    You who make Yourself known in so many stories,
    particularly the story of Jesus of Nazareth,

We thank You for these moments
  shared together in worship,
 for the hope which is given flesh
  in one another,
 for the peace which is the deepest
  longing of our lives.
We pray that we may, now and always,
 remember, name and mourn those who
 suffer from injustice, famine and war,
 and accept all sorrows as our own.
We pray for comfort, compassion and courage
 that we may rededicate ourselves
  to grace and justice and peace
   among all people,
 and prepare to receive the joy of Easter
  into our own stories. Amen.

HYMN: "Lord of All Hopefulness"

BENEDICTION ☦

(With thanks to Rev. Patricia Budd Kepler, pastor of Clarendon Hill Presbyterian Church in Somerville, MA, and Rev. Leslie Norman, pastor of Sanbornton Congregational Church, UCC, in Sanbornton, NH, who helped develop this service.)

Liturgy Of The Passion
(Continued from page 18)

Read Luke 23:26-49.

Dramatic Reading: A Roman Soldier
  Object: Crown of thorns

I was just following orders. It's what I was supposed to do. I'm a soldier. Soldiers follow orders. And now it's over. It's done. He didn't even flinch. They said he could have saved himself. But he didn't. I have never seen anyone die like he did. It was...I don't know...I just don't have the words. He died...well...like...ummm....like a king. Like a real king. (Lay crown of thorns on the altar.)

Hymn: "Were You There?" Verse 5

Prayers of the People

Hymn: "What Wondrous Love Is This"

  Depart in Silence ☦

[1] Ruth Duck & Maren Tirabassi, editors, Touch Holiness, The Pilgrim Press, 1990, p. 59.

The Confession
(Continued from page 32)

something just before I started bragging about being willing to die with him. *(frustrated)* What was it? Why didn't I listen more and talk less? *(peak of his anger and frustration—hits altar rail)*

GIRL: *(frightened...this is all too much for her)* I'd better go before they...

PETER: "Go! Go before..." That's it! Jesus said, "But after I have been RAISED, I will go before you to Galilee..."

GIRL: "Raised"? What did he mean? That's a strange way to describe escaping from the Romans.

PETER: But not a strange way to describe returning from the dead.

GIRL: Raised from the DEAD? But no one...

PETER: He can! I've seen him do it...bring people back from the dead.

GIRL: But himself: could he bring HIMSELF back?

PETER: I don't know. *(already losing the faint ray of hope he held for a moment)* I don't know what to believe anymore. *(turns away briefly, then senses the girl's movement)* Where are you going?

GIRL: To follow.

PETER: Follow who?

GIRL: Follow love. To seek a love that is stronger than fear—even the fears that have controlled my whole life until this moment...to discover a love that might be stronger than death itself. Jesus is filled with that kind of love. I know he is! And his love is calling to me. I must go...

PETER: Go where?

GIRL: Wherever Jesus goes: to prison, to death, to a tomb. I must know: can they kill him? Or can his kind of love conquer fear—conquer death itself? I must know...*(she moves up aisle and out)*

PETER: If it is possible...if his love is truly that great, then there might be hope of forgiveness for me...*(begins to exit, then stops, looks over congregation and speaks to them:)* Hope for ALL of us...

(Exits into darkness. At this point in our service, all lights are lowered and we create a "storm" effect using the sound of wind and flashing lights around the cross erected at the front of the sanctuary. As the "storm" dies away a benediction is pronounced in the darkness, inviting the people to leave in silence. The lights are raised enough to provide safe exit but still retain the feeling of darkness.) ☦

The Way Of The Cross

by Delia Halverson

An adult class in our church gave a gift to the whole congregation on Good Friday. But the big plus was the learning that took place as the committees in the class planned the event. Teachers have realized for years that the greatest learning happens as we prepare. This time the students also learned this truth.

The plan was for a self-directed journey that families or individuals could take, depicting those last hours of Jesus' life. The class also wanted to help persons, in some way, to relate these events to their own lives. This would be done at several locations around the church with construction paper footprints directing the persons from one location to another.

Several weeks before Easter committees were given a section of the last seventy-two hours of Jesus' life. Each committee researched the scriptures, looked for pictures, and located or made items that would symbolize something about their appointed time frame. Each committee turned in a description of how their display would be set up, the scripture that would accompany that display, and any suggestions of ideas of printed information to be read at the display. One person took the material and wrote up a unified format for each display, including a brief description (appropriate for children and adults) of the event, suggestions of what the display represented, reflective thoughts, and suggestions of ways to apply this learning to our lives today. The following is a summary of the display, the reflective questions, and the suggestions for applying it to our lives.

A PLOT UNFOLDS
Judas plots Jesus' arrest.

(Display: Small cross draped in black, picture of Jesus, and bag of gold coins.)

- How do you see the Kingdom of God?
- Who is a part of the Kingdom?
- Is the person who lives in a small shack important to God?
- What about the person who treats you as if you aren't important?
- Do you see the person who cuts you off in traffic as important to God?

A PARTING MEAL
Jesus washes his friends' feet and they share a meal.

(Display: Pitcher, basin, towel, and open sandals. After reviewing the display we moved to a table where we were silently served communion.)

- When did someone do something for you that you didn't expect?
- What can you do for someone else that is beyond what is expected of you? (offer to care for a neighbor's child; tell someone that you like their choice of clothing; hold the door for someone; help neighbors clean their yard or do another family member's chore)

A PLACE TO PRAY
Jesus asked his friends to pray.

(Display: Bench in a garden, picture of Jesus in Gethsemane, clipboard for writing prayer requests, and basket of prayer bookmarks to take for use at home.)

- Write a prayer request you might have on the clip-

board. Read the prayer requests of others and pray for them.
- Do you have a special place at home that you go alone to pray?
- Decide on a time that you can set aside to talk to God each day.

THE ENEMY COMES
Jesus is arrested, and Peter denies knowing Jesus.

(Display: Picture of Jesus bound at the wrists, leather straps, bag of coins, tape recording of Peter's denial with the crowing of the cock.)

- Look at the bag of coins. What in your life might the moneybag represent? Are there things you consider more important than Jesus?
- Feel the leather straps and bind your own hands. Imagine how Jesus must have felt. Remember that Jesus was aware of the physical troubles that lay ahead of him.
- After listening to the recording of Peter's denial, think about times that you find it hard to do as you know Jesus wants you to do.
- When can you help someone else understand how you feel about God?

THE DECISION
Pilate washes his hands.

(Display: In a restroom, a picture of Pilate washing his hands was displayed on the mirror, soap and nice paper guest towels were available beside the sink.)

- Wash your hands slowly, remembering how often we all try to "wash our hands" of responsibilities.
- Ask God for forgiveness. Remember that Jesus has washed us clean by the grace of God.

THEY MOCKED HIM
They placed a scarlet robe and crown of thorns on Jesus and mocked him.

(Display: Picture of Jesus with crown of thorns and scarlet robe, large wooden cross propped on its side, a crown of thorns, and bowl of vinegar with Q-tips.)

- Look at the crown of thorns. Touch the thorns and think how it must have felt. You may place the crown on your head.
- When has someone been unkind because you put your faith first?
- Feel of the cross, lift it. Imagine how heavy it must have been. Would you want to carry it?
- When have you been asked to do something that seemed very hard? Next time, think of Jesus right there with you even if it's hard.
- Take a Q-tip and taste the vinegar.
- When have you suffered pain? Remember Jesus understands our physical pain. When he refused the pain-deadening drug, he experienced what is said to be the most painful death that there is.

AT THE FOOT OF THE CROSS
A game of dice for his garments as Jesus gives his last words. All they saw of importance was his clothing.

(Display: Picture of Jesus on the cross, a crumpled white robe, sandals and pair of dice. Beside it was a large upright cross with a crown of thorns hung over the top and the last words of Jesus were printed on parchment paper and nailed to the cross. There was a recording of the scripture read dramatically.)

- Which is more important to you? people or a new car? a bigger home? a new toy or computer game?
- When have you failed to look for the good in someone else?
- Next time someone tells you, "Oh, you won't like that person," try to find something about the person that you can like. Remember, God loves the person.
- Forgive those who wrong you.

IT IS FINISHED
Jesus accomplished his mission.

(Display: At the chancel of the sanctuary a large wooden cross lay on the steps. There were papers and pencils on the altar rail, a bowl of vinegar and sponge, and a hammer and nails were beside the cross.)

- Take a piece of paper. Write down any sins, fears, concerns, problems or anxieties that you wish to get rid of and then fold the paper over.
- Use the hammer to nail your paper to the cross. Know that you have given Christ those things that you wrote on the paper. Christ helps us carry our problems.

AND WE ARE AN EASTER PEOPLE!
(As we left the sanctuary, we picked up a flyer with this information.)

We call Good Friday "good" because we know what

(Continued on page 38)

Good Friday Vigil

by Maren Tirabassi

A revision of a traditional three-hour Good Friday service can be held early in the evening from 4:00 - 7:00 p.m. People can come and go, knowing that there are four fifteen minute services, each with a particular focus. Some people may come for the entire time, while others may choose one or two services and the quiet prayer which bridges between them. In the course of this early evening worship, all four of the gospel stories of the crucifixion will be read.

The 4:00 p.m. worship focuses on contemporary places of suffering and crucifixion and may use newspaper articles or prayers and poems from the global community. The 5:00 p.m. worship is offered particularly for children and includes an understanding of Good Friday for them. The ideas of sadness, loss and death will perhaps reflect experiences the children have had with the death of friends, relatives or pets. It should avoid language of personal blame for Jesus' execution and should conclude with a clearly verbalized connection of Good Friday with Easter and the empty tomb. The 6:00 p.m. worship is to remember personal friends who have died in the past year, acknowledge the reality of our grief for them and affirm the resurrection in their name. Local church concerns are included in the prayer. The 6:45 p.m. worship gathers up the earlier themes and uses readings and poems that artistically interpret our many feelings about Christ's sacrificial death.

Order of Worship

4:00 p.m.—Opening the Vigil

WORDS OF GATHERING

HYMN: "Rock of Ages, Cleft for Me"

GOOD FRIDAY STORY IN MARK 15

READINGS IN THE SPIRIT OF GOOD FRIDAY
Three or four lay readers can read newspaper articles about hunger, war or other situations throughout the nation and the world where "crucifixion" continues.

PRAYERS FOR OURSELVES AND SUFFERING PEOPLE

HYMN: "Were You There When They Crucified My Lord?" *(first three verses)*

BENEDICTION

TIME OF SILENT PRAYER

5:00 P.M.—Service for Young People

WORDS OF GATHERING

SONG: "Lord of the Dance" *(teach and interpret song as needed)*

STORY: *(for example)* "How the Robin Got a Red Breast"

THE GOOD FRIDAY STORY IN LUKE 23

DISCUSSION: When have we experienced death?

PRAYER, LORD'S PRAYER

STORY: *(for example)* "Caterpillar, Chrysalis, What...?"

BENEDICTION AND PASSING OUT BUTTERFLIES:

Young people can put names on these paper-cut butterflies of people for whose deaths they are sad and return with them on Easter morning to put among the lily display.

TLME OF SILENT PRAYER

6:00 p.m.—A Time for Remembering

WORDS OF GATHERING

HYMN: "On a Hill Far Away"

THE GOOD FRIDAY STORY IN MATTHEW 27

REMEMBERING OF THOSE WHO HAVE DIED

A list of the names found in the record book of our church of those who have died in the last year will be read. There will be a moment of reflective silence, and, if anyone wishes to comment on this person, an opportunity to do so. After each silence, the pastor will say: O God, we give You thanks for this life we shared. The response will be: God, we give You thanks that this person has already entered Easter. A flower will be placed in the vase on the communion table.

After these names have been read, other names will be shared of those we have known in other places or who have been dead longer than this year, but for whom our grief is fresh. For each of these we will offer the thanksgiving.

READING OF PSALM 23

PRAYERS FOR OUR CHURCH

HYMN: "Were You There When They Crucified My Lord?"
(first three verses)

BENEDICTION

TIME OF SILENT PRAYER

6:45 p.m.—Closing the Vigil

WORDS OF GATHERING

HYMN: "When I Survey the Wondrous Cross"

THE GOOD FRIDAY STORY IN JOHN 19
Lay readers may choose poems or prayers reflecting the significance of Good Friday for personal wholeness and grace.

PRAYERS OF CONFESSION, THANKSGIVING AND INTERCESSION

HYMN: "Where You There When They Crucified My Lord?"
(first three verses)

BENEDICTION
Go in God's grace, which even the most brooding Friday cannot shadow, until we meet again in Easter dawn. ✞

The Way Of The Cross
(Continued from page 36)

happened at Easter. We know that God wouldn't let Jesus stay dead. We know that Easter has made a difference in the world.

Reflect on these times the rest of today and tomorrow as you prepare for Easter. The events listed below will also help you to prepare and celebrate Easter.

Tonight: Tenebrae Service—A special service to prepare for Easter.

Tomorrow: Easter Saturday—We encourage you to spend the day preparing yourself and your house for Easter. In reality, Easter is the most important celebration for Christianity. Have simple meals, make the house shine, and prepare yourself! Be ready to welcome the risen Christ on Sunday!

Sunday: Sunrise Service—Look at Easter through the eyes of the disciples.

Easter Worship—Bring a live flower to add to our living cross in celebration of the living Christ. After each service you are invited to join us in front of the cross to release live butterflies, symbolic of Christ coming from the tomb.

Season of Easter—Remember that Easter Sunday is only the beginning of the Easter Season. Easter actually lasts until Pentecost Sunday. Greet your friends and family during that time by wishing them "Happy Easter!" ✞

Good Friday Silence And Poetry

by David Trembley

People who come to Lenten services may well be more ready to be stretched and challenged than are the regular attenders at Sunday morning worship. It would be a shame to give them simply more of the same old thing, which amounts to the role of passive spectators.

Ironically, one worship element which can invite more complete involvement is silence. Superficially, it would seem that silence is the ultimate of passive qualities, but it doesn't work out that way in practice. Silence, in the right places and the right amounts, can create space in which worshipers can hear themselves as well as the Holy Spirit of God.

But silence can be threatening. Too much silence, too soon, will drive people away. It will make them so uncomfortable that they will shut down inside and put up increased defenses. So begin slowly. It is probably best to be very explicit in presenting the innovation. Say something like, "In our Lenten series this year we are going to make a disciplined, consistent effort to seek the blessings and benefits of silence."

Prayer is a good place to start. Two or three minutes of silence in the first prayer is probably enough, and make sure that the organ is not playing. The time can be increased in later services to as much as five minutes or so, but anything longer than five minutes will probably not work until persons are encouraged to reflect upon—and do something with—the silence they have experienced.

Once a congregation has come to appreciate a time of silence in worship, they will begin to demand it. Silence is a time for centering and preparation, and you may well discover, if you introduce silence in worship, that the silence will be broken by the spontaneous, heart-felt prayers of people who are moved by the Holy Spirit to pray aloud.

For some worshipers, silence will become such a powerful element of worship that they will be transformed by the experience. Contemplatives and Quakers, after all, often spend great blocks of time in worshipful silence. Most of us, however, feel the need to "<u>do something</u> with the silence."

One of the most satisfying things to do is create a piece of art.

There are many different ways to combine the activities of worship and art, but for congregations that have been properly prepared, the three-hour service on Good Friday offers an especially powerful possibility. You might, for example, spend an hour in silent meditation (either directed or not; we know a congregation that observed two hours of silence) and then spend the next hour writing a poem.

At first glance, of course, poetry is just as (if not more) threatening as silence. Persons will need to be lead very gently into the possibility of seeing themselves as poets. Here's a simple way to begin. Pass out pens and paper and say, "Now we are going to write a poem. God has blessed us with the gift of the Holy Spirit's presence, and we are now going to make a gift to God."

These instructions assume a congregation which does not see itself as poets. Anyone in the congregation who believes they do not need these instructions should be cheerfully excused and encouraged to follow their own muse. For those who think they do not know how to write a poem, however, this process will yield surprising results.

1. The first key is to **collect images**. Tell the people that the only thing that matters is quantity. The goal is to express, in sense-based language, as many expressions of the experience as the poet can find and get down on paper. Make it clear that issues like sentence structure and spelling are completely beside the point. In fact, writers should try for as brief and non-connected (both grammatically and in terms of continuity of thought) writing as they can manage.

2. Next comes **selection**. Each poet should choose one to three images which seem especially compelling to them. These choices are to be made on the purely subjective basis that "these are the images which seem the most attractive to me."

3. Now comes the **rhythm**. For heaven's sake, don't introduce formal metrical terms. Talk instead of the "beat" of language. There are really only two choices—stressed and unstressed syllables—and these choices arrange themselves in patterns of twos and/or threes. Encourage the poets to play with possible rhythms for their images.

4. Encourage the poets to **compress** their creations as much as they can. Tell them to concentrate on nouns and verbs and get rid of as much modifying material as they can without mortally wounding their creation.

5. Seek some sort of **closure**. For example, if any want to read their poems, encourage them to do so. Find out first what sort of feedback they want, if any. Encourage those who do not want to share publicly to spend some more time on their poem when they get a chance, and offer all who are interested an opportunity in the future to share their creations.

There are abundant resources available for helping persons learn how to write poetry. There is probably, for instance, a group of poets in your community that is eager to offer instruction to fledgling poets. If all else fails, go to your library and get a copy of John Ciardi's How Does a Poem Mean?

Here are two examples of the sort of high-quality poetry which can result from following the simple procedure we have described for creating poetry out of silence.

If one hour of shared silence and one poem make for powerful worship, what about the possibility of extending the experience to something like a Holy Saturday Vigil? The experience might be especially appropriate for a youth group and/or for a group of adolescents and their parents.

When planning an event of this length, of course, significant modifications will need to be made. Consider the following issues.

1. An hour of silence is almost certainly too much for a teenager. Start with ten minutes, and be flexible in terms of building to a duration which works for these participants.

2. Make the poem into a rap, and write it in teams rather than as individuals. Try mixed groups—parents with their offspring, or intergenerational clusters that do not contain members of the same family.

3. Write and stage little dramas based upon the issues which are contained in the meanings of Holy Saturday.

4. Do a visual arts project. A mural on newsprint which has been attached to the wall and finger painting are two suggestive possibilities.

Above all, remember when planning services of great length and novel activities that worshipers will demonstrate a range of willingness and ability to participate. Therefore, consider the possibilities of...
- providing alternative, "more traditional" activities for the hesitant and reluctant participants;
- building in the option to come and go as the participants choose.

For Tom on Maundy Thursday
by Lo-Ann Zhora Trembley

I washed your feet last night with soap and water
   not with tears
  I made my hands a prayer
  I saw the dark hair
    etch its tracery patterns across your instep
    bathing curling toes as your mother must have done
I dried your feet with a terry towel
  not my hair
  Your boney heel filled my cupped palm
I felt a deep, a fleshly scar across the soul and smelled
  anointing balm.

Good Friday Vigil
by Thomas Dale Brown

I watch the line of red threads
An "X" stitched; another—
  Red cross, red blood flowing on
Sunlight dims; traffic roars
These souls hear silence
  Red cross, red blood flowing on
Watch. Pray. Each stitch a cross, a pattern
They seize the cloak of whole cloth. A die is cast;
  another
  Red cross, red blood flowing on
Darkness descends; earth shakes.
Three men hang together
Wait. Know. Wonder. This cross? Death? Savior?
  Red cross, red blood flowing on. ✠

Holy Saturday Communion Meditation

by Joyce DeToni-Hill

Text: *Luke 23:44-24:2*

Meditation:

I like Luke's version of the death of Jesus. The Good Friday account ends with the women watching to see where Christ is laid and then go to prepare the spices. At the end the scripture simply says (in verse 56), "They rested according to the commandment."

And that's where the mystery takes over. There is so much left unsaid. Have you ever wondered what they all were doing on that Holy Saturday? Do you ever wonder where the disciples were at this time? Perhaps they were hiding out. Perhaps they were afraid. Can you see them huddled quietly in a corner in shock, too numb to even make sense of it all? Were they talking nonstop about what they should have done? Did they blame the officials, or even themselves, for what happened?

And what did the women do? The scriptures say that they rested. But did they truly rest? Did they eat? Did they have time to eat a meal while gathering the spices? Did they talk, cry, embrace?

And do you ever wonder what God was doing on that Holy Saturday? GOD WAS WORKING.

Like glass shattered on the kitchen floor, God was sweeping up the Good Friday mess and saying, "Now what am I going to do with this!?" And that mess God swept was ugly. It consisted of a lot of failures.

Politics failed the people and Jesus. Religion was devalued and abused in the face of innocence. That ugly mess contained disappointments, guilt, betrayal and sin.

But God didn't throw that mess away. Rather, God went to work melting, molding and reshaping it into a new creation. Holy Saturday is a sacred space. It is like a chrysalis where a worm is melted down completely into a colorfully winged insect.

Holy Saturday is like the dark warm womb in which God works lovingly to knit a new being, cell by cell. We don't know the outcome, but we know it will be a miracle.

Like the chrysalis and the womb, God took Good Friday and created a NEW THING. We are people of the Word. We participate in Christ's story. If we are to be the Good Friday people standing at the foot of the cross, and if we are to be Easter people singing, "Every Morning is Easter Morning From Now On," then we must also see ourselves as the Holy Saturday people as well.

As you come forward for communion, I invite you to bring your disillusionments, your broken dreams, your paralyzing failures, and as community we will share, we will restore, and indeed, we will redeem.

Come, bring your brokenness, and offer this to Christ. Receive in those same hands the body that was broken, but now through the resurrection is the new creation. Receive the blood that was spilled but now offers new life.

HOLY SATURDAY PEOPLE, COME WITH EXPECTATION, FOR GOD IS ABOUT TO DO A NEW THING. ✞

Lent And Easter Packets

by Deborah Payden

It is important to connect the celebration of Lent and Easter that takes place in church with daily family life. Resources are needed for families to help them reflect upon and celebrate these seasons at home. One such resource is a Lent or Easter packet.

These packets are large envelopes (8 1/2" by 11"), containing a variety of activities and suggestions for families to use during the Lent and Easter seasons. On the outside of the envelope is information about the particular season, the reason for the packets and a list of its contents. The activities, ideas and suggestions in the envelopes are designed for a variety of ages within the family. The name of each family is written at the top of the envelope. The Lent packets are handed out in church on the Sunday prior to Ash Wednesday. The Easter packets are handed out to families following worship on Easter Sunday.

For making the assembly of these packets easier, have the Christian Education Committee or some other church group divide up the responsibility for gathering, obtaining, copying and designing the various activities for the envelope. (This becomes a good way to educate about the Lent and Easter season as well.) Put the envelopes together at a Committee meeting, or during a special time set aside for this assembly.

Below is a list of possible activities to include in such a packet. Perhaps your church can think of others.

Lenten Packet

- Daily scripture readings of a Gospel for the family
- Information about the tradition and a recipe for baking pretzels
- Ideas for a Lenten mission project, or a calendar for Lenten sacrifice
- Ideas for prayer
- Seeds to plant
- Craft sticks and yarn to make Lenten crosses Crossword and Word search puzzles for Lent Activities for communion education
- Symbols for Lent and Holy week to be used to make a family mobile or banner
- Lenten liturgies for home use

Easter Packet

- Symbol sheet for Eastertide
- Paper cross pattern for use in making a resurrection cross (with directions for cutting magazine pictures out to make a collage)
- Butterfly stickers
- Easter bread recipes
- Easter word search and crossword puzzles
- Suggestions for making Easter cards for home-bound individuals
- Directions for making an Easter windsock from construction crepe paper
- Directions for making a mosaic out of broken colored Easter egg shells of an Easter symbol
- Easter liturgy for the home ✠

The Questions Of Mark

by Robert G. Davidson

What were the questions which the author of the Gospel of Mark was trying to answer with the writing of his gospel?

The Gospel According to Mark was the first of the four gospels to be written. It is believed to have been written around 70 A.D., some 35 years after the resurrection event of Jesus Christ. Its author introduced to the Roman world a type of popular literature previously unknown. Here for the first time the words and deeds of Jesus were remembered and proclaimed in a written form. Mark was not trying to set down a formal historical treatise nor a biography of Jesus, but a proclamation. The author's intention is clearly paraphrased in the opening line of his Gospel, "The beginning of the preaching of the good news of Jesus Christ." What follows is a narrative which focuses on a crisis—the death of Jesus as the Christ.

:emt is a special time of meditation and study. Through these forty days, excluding Sundays, we enter Jesus' story as it is shared with us in the Gospel of Mark. Try and place yourself back in time, think about the questions which the people were raising about this man Jesus around 70 A.D. Put yourself in Mark's place. How would you answer the questions which the people were asking about Jesus?

Take some time and read the Gospel of Mark straight through—it will take about two hours. During the forty days of Lent read the suggested passages and meditate on each one daily, and relate it to your daily life experiences and relationships with other people. You may wish to write down notes and personal thoughts in a separate journal. You might enter into a shared conversation with another member of your family or a friend daily. Think about Mark's questions, raise your own, let them become a part of your life today.

What Is The Theme Of Mark's Gospel?

ASH WEDNESDAY—DAY 1
   What is the theme of this Gospel? Ch. 1:1. Beginning Ash Wednesday, what better day to think about the message God sent to humankind through Jesus; a historical event which introduced a new course of action on the part of God. What kind of action did God take? What was new about it? Read this opening verse in Mark several times. Think about the meaning of each word.

THURSDAY—DAY 2
   Who is this man in the wilderness? Ch. 1: 4-8. John the Baptist appeared in the wilderness, preaching a baptism of repentance. Repent means changing your ways, turning around. For most of us, as we think back over a day, there are things we might have said or done that we wish we might change or had handled in a different way. How can you not make the same mistakes tomorrow?

FRIDAY—DAY 3
   Why does Jesus go off to be alone? Ch. 1:9-11. Jesus goes off into the wilderness in order to consider the possibilities which lay before him. He is confronted with many temptations. It is this confrontation which is itself important, since it is sustained throughout Jesus' ministry. We are confronted with temptations throughout our lives. How do you cope with temptations in your everyday life?

SATURDAY— DAY 4
   Is Jesus confronted with a decision? Ch. 1:12-13. Jesus is confronted with his ministry, his mission in life. He was sorting through his thoughts, he was trying to make a decision about the things he must do. Jesus thinks through the decisions he was about to make which were going to effect the rest of his life. Do we take time to think through

how our life is going- past decisions and comments we may have made to ourselves and to others? Are we looking forward to the future? How do you face the temptation of not accepting the responsibilities of being followers of Jesus?

Why And Where Does Jesus' Ministry Begin?

MONDAY—DAY 5
Where does his ministry begin? Ch. 1:14-15. Jesus' ministry does not begin until John the Baptist is arrested. At this time Jesus declares that the critical moment has come: God begins to act in a new and decisive way. He announces that the Kingdom of God is at hand. Are we called to repent, to change our ways? Do we all have a personal ministry? When does your ministry, as a Christian, begin? With the beginning of each new day?

TUESDAY—DAY 6
Who does he call to be disciples? Ch. 1:16-20. Jesus is calling people to be part of the inbreaking kingdom. Who is this man called Jesus who is extending a call to others to follow him? Why should they even consider such a call? How would you have responded if you were Peter or Andrew or John? How would you respond today if Jesus stood in front of you and extended his call to you, knowing that it would mean leaving your family, job, friends, etc.?

WEDNESDAY—DAY 7
Is Jesus someone special? Ch. 1:21-28. Those who heard Jesus, knew this man taught with a great deal of authority. In the presence of Jesus, men and women were disturbed. Jesus wanted them to be more than they were at the present time. He was calling them to become someone different than they had ever thought of being. Does Jesus disturb you today? How? What does he want _you_ to become?

THURSDAY—DAY 8
How did he heal the sick? Ch. 1:32-34. The sick people were brought to Jesus to be healed and Jesus reached out to them, but often he fulfilled a need for which that a person was not aware or seeking assistance. Jesus gave the ill people a new way of understanding their illness and their needs. He knows your real needs today, but will ~ let him help you? Do you really want God to know you so well?

FRIDAY—DAY 9
Did Jesus find strength in solitude? Ch. 1:35-39. Jesus left to find a place of solitude. He did this often throughout his ministry. He went off by himself to talk and listen to God. This time he has to make a decision whether to stay or leave Capernaum. Do we take time to be alone when considering important decisions and share with God? Do we take time to listen to God's response? Are you always receptive to God's response? Are _you_ afraid that God will ask you to do that which you don't really want to do?

SATURDAY—DAY 10
How could this man cause controversy? Ch. 2:1-3:6. Jesus and his teachings were causing conflict in Galilee. The five narratives found here share in common the element of controversy. Jesus and his disciples were being openly challenged. How often are you challenged because of a stand you take as a follower of Jesus as a Christian?

Why Did Jesus Withdraw To The Sea?

MONDAY—DAY 11
Should Rome be concerned about Jesus? Ch. 3:7-12. Jesus withdrew to the sea to get away from the crowds. The large crowds which came to hear him were also drawing unwanted attention. The Roman rulers were becoming concerned about who this man Jesus was and why was he gathering crowds of people. Why should Jesus' message be causing such concern? Would it cause such concern today?

TUESDAY—DAY 12
Who are the followers of Jesus? Ch. 3:13-19a. Jesus continued to call others to be disciples until he had selected twelve. He had men from various backgrounds and interests: several fishermen, a tax collector, a young person, several older men, quiet persons, one with a temper; but all dedicated to Jesus' call. If you were called upon to describe what discipleship meant as a Christian, what would _you_ say?

WEDNESDAY—DAY 13
What was the character of Jesus' family? Ch. 3:19b-35. Who are the members of Jesus' family? In these passages Jesus' family comes to where he is teaching. He asks the question, "Who are my mother and my brothers?" His response is, "Whoever does the will of God." As you live day to day, are _you_ doing the will of God? Are you part of Jesus' family?

Why Did Jesus Use Parables In Teaching About The Kingdom Of God?

THURSDAY—DAY 14
Why did Jesus use parables? Ch. 4:1-9. The parable was Jesus' number one way of teaching. What is a parable? To understand a parable you have to think about it. You have to relate it to your life. The message within the parable is not obvious to the person who hear it. What does this parable of the sower say to you? What kind of ground have you been? Rocky? Fertile? Can you write a contemporary parable?

FRIDAY—DAY 15
Do we take things too literally? Ch. 4:10-12. We are taught today to take everything literally. It is difficult for us to comprehend a pictorial image as they did when these stories were told verbally. We need to spend time trying to find meaning in this story. What is Jesus saying here, that you hear and see but do not respond?

SATURDAY—DAY 16
What kind of ground are you? Ch. 4: 13-20. Think back to a couple of days ago and recall how you interpreted the parable of the sower. Now read today's passage. What would you change about your previous interpretation? What did you learn? How would you explain the parable of the sower to another person?

MONDAY—DAY 17
Can we change? Ch. 4:26-29. Jesus used many stories and parables related to the concept of growth, the idea of change. We are all in the process of growth and change; this is part of IKe. What happens when we feel that we have arrived, when we feel that we have all the answers? Do you know people who give the impression of "knowing it all"? Have they stopped growing? Have you?

TUESDAY—DAY 18
What is the kingdom of God? Ch. 4:30-32. Have you ever seen a mustard seed? A mustard seed is very small, but it can produce a very large bush. Thinking about this parable, how would you describe the kingdom of God? How would you relate this story of the mustard seed to the kingdom of God? How would you define the kingdom of God to another person?

What Were Some Of The Other Events In Galilee?

WEDNESDAY—DAY 19
Can you reach out to a person in need? Ch. 5:1-20. Read this narrative several times carefully. Picture the scene in your mind—the fear in the crowd, the feelings the Gerasene man is experiencing, and Jesus reaching out to this man. Try and sense the drama taking place between this man and Jesus. It is very hard for us to reach out to someone we don't want to associate with or even be near. What can you learn from this narrative, and hopefully put into practice?

THURSDAY—DAY 20
Is support easy to give? Ch. 6:1-6a. Jesus is facing rejection! How strange it seems that we find rejection for the good we try to do from the very people we feel should be supporting us and giving us the strongest love as we reach out to others to share the love of God. Have you ever let someone down that you should have been supporting? How do you think they felt?

FRIDAY—DAY 21
Can you share the "good news"? Ch. 6:6b-13. Jesus had been teaching and instructing his disciples for months, and now the time had come for them to reach out and share the "good news" with others. Have you, as a disciple of Jesus, gone out to share the "good news" with those around you? What would you say? What would you do?

Why Did Jesus Feel He Should Leave Galilee?

SATURDAY—DAY 22
Do you often act too soon? Ch. 6:30-34. Have you ever gone off to be alone? There were the crowds, people seeking help, the disciples asking deep, searching questions, time running short-all these things were coming at Jesus. The days were not long enough to get everything done. Jesus needed time and a lonely place to pull his thoughts together, to sort things through with his disciples. Do you take time to sit down with a friend and sort things through in shared conversation?

MONDAY—DAY 23
What is this bread of life? Ch. 6:35-44. There are many interpretations of this narrative. Was Jesus feeding

their bodies or their souls? How did Jesus manifest the food which all the people needed? Did the abundance of food appear from everyone sharing what they had with others? If so, would you call this a miracle? Would this be a greater miracle than just having the food appear in some mysterious way? How do you share?

TUESDAY—DAY 24
Are we all equal? Ch. 7:24-30. Who was Jesus' message for? His message was for all people it was for the Gentile and the Jew. He was saying that all people were equal in God's sight. Does that include the aging, the homeless, the criminal, and the powerful? In your everyday life. how can you apply that idea?

WEDNESDAY—DAY 25
Are we always seeking a new sign? Ch. 8:11-13. What is a sign? How would you define a sign? What would a sign have to be in order for you to believe in it? We are always looking for a sign. If we do not see one, we procrastinate and put off making important decisions or commitments. What are you putting off in your life while you are waiting for a sign? What would a sign mean to you and your life in the near future?

THURSDAY—DAY 26
Do we really want to understand? Ch. 8:14-21. Jesus concludes this passage with the phrase, "Do you not yet understand?" We have heard Jesus' teachings over and over again through the years. But how often have you sat down and really tried to think one of them through? Are they as complex and complicated as you think? Or are they pretty simple, but make your life complicated if you take them seriously?

FRIDAY—DAY 27
What did this man see? Ch. 8:22-26. That is a question we all should ponder. The man was blind, then he could see. Jesus made him whole. How often are we blind and cannot see that we need to reach out to a loved one, or cannot see the beauty of God's great earth, or take time to see a rose at the same time? Do you really want to see and understand?

SATURDAY—DAY 28
Did they realize who he was? Ch. 8:27-30. In this passage we find a turning point in the Gospel of Mark. Up to this point we are not sure as to who Jesus is, but here it is made clear as Peter makes his confession **"You are the Christ."** How has this great statement by Peter made a discernible difference in your life?

Why Did Jesus Believe He Should Go To Jerusalem?

MONDAY—DAY 29
How strong is your unbelief? Ch. 9:14-29. "I believe; help my unbelief!" If they were put on a scale, which would tip the scale down, our belief or our unbelief? What do you believe in? Is it hard to have faith in anything in our society today? Everything seems to be shaded gray. Is your believe in God and what He can do also shaded gray?

TUESDAY—DAY 30
Who are the great? Ch. 9:33-37. We are always seeking greatness in some way in our society-in work, in sports, in education, and so forth. There are many people who seem to feel that they are owed the place of being first-first in line, first to cross the line. But what did Jesus say here? What meaning does it have to you in this passage?

WEDNESDAY—DAY 31
How complex is Jesus' message? Ch. 10:13-16. In this passage of the blessing of the children what was Jesus saying? What was he trying to communicate to those who were listening? Jesus said to receive the kingdom of God as a child. That is something to think about. Do you think that over the years and even centuries we have made Jesus' basic teachings too complicated? Is the Christian message pretty simple? Define it?

THURSDAY—DAY 32
Can you buy into the kingdom of God? Ch. 10:17-27. Jesus told the rich young man to give up all his possessions if he wanted to have eternal life. That is a pretty hard concept for most of us to consider. This would mean a radical change in our life styles. Does Jesus want you to look within yourself, to your attitudes, beliefs and faith?

FRIDAY—DAY 33
Why must Jesus go to Jerusalem? Ch. 10:32-34. Jesus realized that he must go to Jerusalem and he knew there were those there who wanted him to be put to death. Did he believe that he could escape those who sought to do him harm? Did he believe there were other people in Jerusalem who must hear the good news of God he was preaching? We are all called to make hard decisions, to do things that we do not want to do. How well do you handle this kind of responsibility?

SATURDAY—DAY 34
What is your faith like? Ch. 10:46-52. If you read this passage with care you will realize that the blind man began with a need, went on to express gratitude, and finished with a deep loyalty. Does the man have loyalty to Jesus because he has gained visual sight, or has he gained new insight into the meaning of life? Has your faith in Jesus helped you to gain insight into your life and added meaning to it?

Did The People In Jerusalem Respond To Jesus' Ministry?

MONDAY—DAY 35
Was he facing death? Ch. 11:1-11. Jesus arrived at the gates to Jerusalem. We can picture in our mind the triumphant scene as Jesus entered Jerusalem. The crowds cheered him on, there was great expectation. The people were with Jesus. He was a winner! We find it easy to be for a winner. But what position do we take when the going gets tough? What happened to all the crowds a few days later, on Friday? Do you jump ship easily when things don't look rosy?

TUESDAY—DAY 36
Why do they seek Jesus? Ch. 14: 1-2. When person seems to be successful there are people supporting him. But there also seems to be a group of individuals who want to pull him down and destroy him. Some of the Jewish religious leaders wanted to seize Jesus. Pilate was concerned about this man, Jesus, and the crowds which gathered about him. Self-interests became a way of life. How do you respond to people and their drive to achieve their personal self-interests?

WEDNESDAY—DAY 37
Why did Judas do it? Ch. 14:10-11. How could Judas, a loyal follower, betray Jesus? Judas was a man who wanted things his way. He wanted Jesus to use his power in a military way, so he was trying to push Jesus into action. He did not understand God's message which Jesus had been sharing. Are you always willing to do it God's way?

THURSDAY—DAY 38
Did the common meal become something more? Ch. 14:22-26. Within just a few years following the resurrection event a common meal became an institution. What joy we find as we gather about a table with family and friends sharing a common meal. What is there about fellowship and communion with others that makes you feel good especially while sharing a common meal?

FRIDAY—DAY 39
How could Peter deny Jesus? Ch. 14:66-72. How could a person do this to another person? It becomes so easy to look down on Peter at this point and say, "How could you have done this deed?" But what if you were in Peters place that night? How would you have responded that night? How would or do you respond today?

SATURDAY—DAY 40
How lonely is this moment? Ch. 15:42-47. This was a lonely and hurting period of time for the disciples and followers of Jesus. We all know the feelings of standing by a grave, experiencing those searching feelings. We ask the question, what does life mean? There was yesterday which you remember, today which you are experiencing, and tomorrow. . . ?

Did God Act In Human History?

EASTER SUNDAY
What joy is there in the Easter message? Ch. 16:1-8. Today we remember an event which changed the course of human history. We may comprehend only a small portion of the total meaning of the Easter event, but we do understand that God stepped into our world and changed the course of human life. God has extended a call to each one of us personally. Let us respond to God's call and celebrate this Easter day with great joy! ✞

A Blossoming Cross

by Mary Jo Shannon

Our church has developed a concrete example to symbolize the transformation of the cross of Good Friday and the crucifixion to the glorious symbol of Easter Sunday and resurrection. A plywood cross, approximately 3' x 2' was constructed with a hinged easel to permit it to stand freely.

Holes (1/4") were drilled through the wood, approximately 2" apart. This empty cross, draped with black cloth, stood at the entrance to the sanctuary during the Service of Darkness on Good Friday.

Notices were printed in the church bulletin for the last two Sundays in Lent, requesting children (and adults!) to bring fresh flowers on Easter Sunday to adorn the cross. Whatever was blooming would be acceptable.

On Easter Sunday, two adults were present to help place the stems in the holes. Experience has taught us this works better, since some children are too short to reach the top, and since the two adults can distribute the flowers more evenly to assure coverage.

By the time the worship service began, the cross was a glorious, colorful and sweet-smelling vision of daffodils, lilacs, tulips, azaleas and forsythia.

Originally, this project was tried as part of the worship service. The empty cross was displayed in the chancel and children came forward to fill it with flowers. Although a meaningful act of worship, it was much too time-consuming, especially during an Easter service already filled with special music. We found the method described here to be much simpler. The congregation also appreciated the opportunity to see the cross up close.

Our flower cross has become a meaningful tradition at Raleigh Court Presbyterian Church, and the entire congregation looks forward to this opportunity to symbolize the Good News of the resurrection. ✞

Readings For Lent

by Ann Wiggins

Do you want an interesting but simple way to involve your church in Lenten readings? Invite members to write a daily devotional booklet.

WHY? People are very interested in Bible readings when the comments are written by someone they know. Therefore, the booklets tend to be read more often that those that are commercially produced.

WHO? This project can easily be adapted so that it can be prepared by a few people or by a large group. It can be a special project for a youth group, seniors' group or church school class. It can also be prepared in a small church by people of all ages.

HOW DO WE GET STARTED? To get started, just follow a few simple steps.

1. Select a scripture reading for each day of Lent. It is often effective to select a theme to carry out. An obvious theme would be readings from the final days of Jesus. However, many other topics can also be used. One possible theme is "Through the Bible". Suggested readings are listed below:

- Creation: Genesis 1:1-2:4
- Creation of Man and Woman: Genesis 2:4-2:25
- The Flood: Genesis 6:5-8:15
- The Call of Abram: Genesis 12:1-9
- Abraham and Isaac: Genesis 22:9-14
- Jacob's Ladder: Genesis 28:10-17
- Moses in the Bulrushes: Exodus 2:1-10
- Moses and the Burning Bush: Exodus 3:1-22
- The Ten Commandments: Exodus 20:1-17, Deuteronomy 5:1-21
- Joshua and the Battle of Jerico: Joshua 6:1-20
- Call of Samuel: 1 Sam. 3:1-4:1
- Anointing of David: 1 Sam. 9:15-10:1
- David and Goliath: 1 Sam. 17:1-54
- The Shepherd Psalm: Psalm 23
- The Voice of the Lord Psalm: Psalm 29
- Advice From Proverbs: Proverbs 10:7, 10:12
- Advice From Proverbs: Proverbs 10:15, 10:20
- Test of Solomon's Wisdom: 1 Kings 3:3-28
- Isaiah: Isaiah 9:1-7
- The Fiery Furnace: Daniel 3:1-30
- The Birth of Jesus: Matthew 1:18-25
- Baptism of Jesus: Matthew 3:13-17
- Plucking Grain of the Sabbath: Luke 6:1-5
- The Golden Rule: Matthew 7:12
- The Great Commandment: Matthew 22:36-40
- Healing the Ten Lepers: Luke 17:11-19
- The Widow's Mite: Mark 12:41-44
- Lazarus and the Rich Man: Luke 16:19-31
- The Lost Sheep: Luke 15:3-7
- Laborers in the Vineyard: Matthew 20:1-15
- Calming the Storm: Mark 4:36-41
- Entry into Jerusalem: Matthew 21:1-11
- The Last Supper: Matthew 26:17-29
- Garden of Gethsemane: Matthew 26:36-46
- Arrest of Jesus: Matthw 26:47-56
- The Crucifixion: Luke 23:44-49
- The Resurrection: Luke 24:1-11
- Pentecost: Acts 2:1-4
- Paul's Conversion: Acts 9:1-9
- God Wipes All Tears: Rev. 7:9-14

Please note this includes a reading for each of the traditional 40 days of Lent, which DOES NOT include Sundays. Sundays are not counted in the penitential season of Lent because in liturgical churches Christ's resurrection is celebrated each Sunday. If you wish, you may easily add a

(Continued on page 110)

An Abstinence Game For The Family

by Christie L. Jenkins

Lent has traditionally been a time of denying oneself and making sacrifices. This denial can be seen as a way to learn self-control, but it is also a means of learning to live a life in service to others—of making the kingdom of God more manifest.

The following activity is one that the whole family can participate in. It should be something the whole family *wants* to do. It should not become another area of conflict between parents and children. Discuss the activity fully before participating.

Rather than giving up one thing for Lent, make the abstaining more variable—one day give up drinking soda, another day give up cookies, etc. What to abstain from on any given day is chosen at random and in effect becomes something of a game, albeit a serious one.

You will need two small boxes which can be decorated with various symbols appropriate to the season. You will also need 40-60 small pieces of paper. Write down non-essential food items commonly found in your kitchen—cookies, candy, soda, potato chips, gum, etc. These are the food items to abstain from. Leave some slips blank; these are days of no abstention. (For a family with very young children, leave more slips blank; with older children, leave fewer blank.) Place the slips of paper in one of the boxes.

Beginning on Ash Wednesday, draw one slip of paper from the box each day. Let the children take turns. The slip might be drawn the evening before for the following day. Whatever is on the slip is abstained from for that day. Calculate (roughly) how much money is saved by everyone not eating that particular food for the day and place this money in the other small box.

Donate the money to a worthy cause (maybe two), preferably an organization that works with children so the youngsters have the knowledge that they are helping other children. Choose an organization that lets the children feel that their contribution makes a difference—a big difference. A good example is UNICEF*. Small donations to this organization go a long way. For 4 cents UNICEF can provide enough doses of vitamin A for one child for one year. (In the spring of 1995 one child was still dying of vitamin A deficiency every minute.) And UNICEF is only one example of what can be accomplished with mere pennies.

About half-way through Lent, sit down as a family and see how you are doing. If you have slacked off a bit, increase your resolve for the second half of Lent. Discuss why you are doing this. Discuss the difficulties in giving up even simple things for short periods. What are you all learning about yourselves?

On Holy Saturday, as part of the preparation for Easter on the following day, count out the money, make out the check for the organization you have chosen, and mail it. Knowing that in a pale imitation of Christ's sacrifice, your sacrifice, too, has made God more present in the world. ☥

*United Nations Children's Fund, 3 United Nations Plaza, New York, NY 10017, 212-326-7000.

Telling Stories During Lent

by Elaine Ward

The Lenten season closes with Easter worship and celebration.

Easter is a story, a mosaic of stories, a confused story of an empty tomb. One account says Mary Magdalene was there first, alone. Another says that she came with Mary, the mother of James and Joanna. One account includes Peter and the beloved disciple. Matthew mentions fear and joy. Because it is confused and varied, it carries the ring of truth, for such is life here and now, as we know and experience it. It is the way the gospel writers experienced the power of the presence of Jesus post-resurrection.

Life in Lent is a story of death, and above all, resurrection, the story of the drama of God's love. Such a story is a compass for following "the way" of Jesus.

The season of Lent is the season of sacred stories. Telling stories during Lent gives substance to our hopes and fears, our loves and hates, our faith and doubt, the good and evil in our lives. Stories are our inner selves speaking the language of the imagination.

Stories are the way we reveal who we are and what we love and value. They grow out of our lives and nourish our lives. Some reveal God hiding in our lives, for that is where we find God.

Lent is a time for remembering the stories of Jesus' happy entrance into Jerusalem on Palm Sunday, of his Last Supper with his friends, of his trials before Annas and Pilate, the horror of his crucifixion, and the glory of his resurrection. They invite us to identify.

Jesus told stories because he wanted his friends to remember.

In <u>Story Journey</u>, Tom Boomershine tells Richard Rice's story of his congregation's "forget-me-not," their remembrance of the story:

"Our group began meeting about eight weeks before Easter. After the first meetings, we agreed that one person in the group would learn the story and tell it in worship for the scripture lesson each week during Lent...The response of the congregation to the telling of the stories was extremely positive, which provided a high degree of incentive for the group. People were excited to see other lay persons telling the stories from memory. They also found the lessons more alive, which in turn helped my preaching. Sometime around the middle of Lent, I proposed to the group that we would tell the entire passion narrative for the Good Friday service. At first, people were reluctant and thoroughly frightened. But when I made it clear that they would only have to tell the stories they had already learned and I would do the rest, they were finally more than willing to do it.

"On Good Friday we rearranged the pews so that the congregation was gathered around us in a rough semi-circle, with the group seated on a bench facing them. We began by singing two passion hymns and then we simply told the story. There were two other hymns during the telling of the story. As the story progressed, the congregation became more and more deeply involved. By the end there was a primary sense of the holiness and the reality of Jesus' death. It was the most meaningful Good Friday service we have ever had. The people were so appreciative and asked that we tell the story every year.

"This experience has made me aware of the power of the story when it is simply told. No sermon could have been more powerful than that story. And the people who told the story have become far more committed leaders in the life of the congregation. Telling the story changed them. It is clear to me that telling the biblical stories introduces a whole new element of meaning that has simply not been present before in the way we have used the scriptures."

Stories speak to the head and the heart to cause us to feel, as well as think. In <u>The Stick Stories</u>[1], Margie Brown tells the story of Mary Magdalene speaking to Jesus:

"Jesus! Jesus, it's me, Mary Magdalene! I'm still here. All the others have gone, but I'm still here.

"Jesus, I don't know what to do! I don't know what to say...What? Are you thirsty? Can I get you a coke or something? I don't know what...

"Jesus, don't die. Please don't die. If you die, then I want to die too. If you die, then I want to...Ouch! A splinter..."

Children like stories about animals, in which they can "overhear" the story of love and sacrifice, and grow into the story of Jesus Christ's giving his life for others.

Once upon a time the man-in-the-moon looked down on earth and saw a rabbit, a monkey and a fox warming themselves around a fire and sharing their supper together, for they were good friends.

The moon said to the stars, "It is time for me to disappear. I will take a trip to earth." The moon said good-bye to the stars because he had an idea. With all the time he had to think through the eons and eons of time, and being very curious, with much imagination, he often wondered which of the three, the rabbit, the monkey or the cow, was the kindest.

Wanting to know but not wanting them to know him, he changed himself into an old and poor beggar. "Please help me," cried the beggar, as he approached the three friends, "I am soooo hungry!"

"How sad," said the three friends, hurrying off to find food for the poor man. The monkey quickly found some bananas in a tree, the fox caught a fish in the brook nearby, but the rabbit could not find any food for the poor man.

Tears filled the rabbit's eyes, but he knew that feeling sorry would not feed the hungry man, so he used his imagination and his thinking and soon he had an idea and a plan. "Mr. Monkey, would you gather some firewood for me?" asked the rabbit. "And Mr. Fox, would you make me a fire with the wood?"

They were friends, so they did as the rabbit asked, and soon the fire burned brightly. The rabbit said to the beggar, "I do not have any food to share with you, but I will give you all that I have. When I am cooked, you may eat me."

The rabbit was about to jump into the fire, when the beggar, the man-in-the-moon cried, "No! You are very kind, but do not harm yourself."

The three friends were amazed as the poor man changed into the man-in-the-moon. "You are the kindest animal I have ever met," he said to the rabbit. "I will take you up into the sky to live with me."

So he did and that is why some nights when you look up at the moon and it is shining brightly, you can see the rabbit, the kindest of them all, for he was the one willing to give his own life to help another live.

"Stepka and the Magic Fire" is a Russian Easter legend:[2]

In the days of the Tzars the people were poor. The harvest was bad. The Cossacks frightened and stole from the peasants, and of all the peasants Stepka had the least of all. Stepka and his three daughters lived on water and brown bread from the New Year until the Nativity.

The people were very poor but on Easter Eve they lit their homes with Easter candles and ran from house to house, shouting, "Christ is risen! He is risen indeed!"

Stepka, however, did not join the others. He had no light and he put his children to bed hungry, with a song on his lips and a pain in his heart. Tomorrow was Easter! From the cupboard Stepka took a box of old Easter candles, but he had no fire to light them. Though too proud to beg, for his children he said, "Give me a light for my Easter candles."

The people instead sent him away with the words, "Christ is risen! He is risen indeed!"

Stepka plodded home, his stomach empty, his heart aching, but his eyes alert when he saw the fires, for he believed them to be Cossacks attacking his village.

Stepka approached the fires slowly, cautiously, yet the sounds of joy coming from the camp made him feel welcome, and as he neared he could hear the cries, "Christ is risen!"

Stepka too now cried, "Christ is risen!"

"He is risen indeed!" said one of the men by the fire.

With such a welcome Stepka asked for a light and they replied, "Help yourself." It was then Stepka realized that he had brought nothing in which to carry the fire.

"Use your coat!" they said, as they threw blazing wood onto his coat.

"Stop! Stop!" cried Stepka. Then Stepka stopped...for the fire burned not a thread of his coat.

Stepka could not believe it, but it was true!

When Stepka pushed open the door of his small hut, he lighted the candles and called to his children. When the children saw the lighted candles, their smiles were his reward.

Yet this was not the only reward or surprise, for his coat on the table was full of...gold coins. Stepka wept and prayed and laughed and prayed, and when his nosey neighbors heard the noise, they looked into the window and cried, "Where did you get this fortune?"

Stepka told them of the charcoal-burners. The villagers raced away. The charcoal-burners were surprised when they came, but they placed coals on their coats as they asked.

Rather than turning to gold, however, their coats began to burn, blisters stung their hands, and they raised their fists in pain and anger, which became cries of astonishment, for the strangers disappeared.

The villagers were sad, but Stepka became the richest man around and his door was always open to the poor. Every Easter Eve Stepka invited the poor, one and all, to share his Easter meal. And in time the little village became known as...Stepka.

There is an old African tale that tells:

Moon had a message for man and woman and called Insect to come and carry the message to earth. The message of Moon was, "As I die, and in dying, live, so you in dying will live also."

Insect took the message of Moon to earth and on the way met Hare. "Where are you going?" asked Hare.

"I have a message from Moon to man and woman. Moon said, "As I die, and in dying, live again, so you in dying will live also."

"Insect, you are slow. Let me take it," said Hare, and Insect gave the message to Hare.

Hare ran off fast and in his hurry, when he found man and woman, said, "Moon has sent you a message that in dying, Moon dies, so you too in dying shall perish."

When Moon heard what Hare had said, Moon was angry and took a stick and hit Hare on the nose. And that is why hares have split noses and men and women think that when they die, they perish.

What we live by we die by. What we think by we live by. The biblical stories were told long before they were collected. They were told and retold long before they were frozen in print. The storyteller's intent is to take stories from the printed page and breathe the story alive.

In breathing the story alive the storyteller puts into the story sounds, body movements, gestures, facial expressions and pauses that cause a story to live. The storyteller gives the characters form and flesh through the speaking of the word. This Lent tell stories! ✞

Borrow from the library or buy Easter books for reading, such as:

Easter Chimes, Stories for Easter and the Spring Season, selected by Wilhelmina Harper, E.P. Dutton, N.Y., 1965

Lillies, Rabbits, and Painted Eggs, Edna Barth, Clarion, NY, 1970.

Hope for the Flowers, Trina Paulus, Paulist Press, Paramus, NJ, 1972.

The Ragman and Other Cries of Faith, Walter Wangerin, Harper & Row, NY, 1984.

New Testament Stories, Elaine M. Ward, Educational Ministries, Prescott, AZ, 1984.

For children's stories, see Ash Wednesday to Easter, as well as the six-week curriculum for adults, Lent, Season of Sacred Stories, with stories for telling during Lent (both by Educational Ministries, Inc.).

[1] Margie Brown, The Stick Stories (Saratoga, CA: Resources Publications, 1982).
[2] Dorothy Van Woerkom, Stepka and the Magic Fire (St. Louis: Concordia, 1974).

Stones

by Don Hartman

Matthew 4:3: "If you are God's Son, order these stones to turn into bread." (TEV)

Temptations wait
in the crusted, hard core
of stones—
temptations that
laugh and weep
"Make us more than we are,
or less."
Dissatisfied with merely being,
stones
seem solid and
unchangeable,
and yet
stones
move endlessly
below the crust
and from the core.
They build monuments
and temples
and prisons;
they crumble
into dust and ashes,
becoming the basic particles
from which non-living
living and we
are made.
We overestimate
the edifaces
of stones—
the monuments,
temples,
and prisons.
These crumble and fall
with time
proving the power
of temptations
to make stones
more than they are.

We underestimate
the particles of stone—
the basic elements
of dust and ashes.
These come together and rise up
bursting through temptations
to make stones
less than they are.
It remains
the nature of stones
to embody such
temptations
—never what they seem
—always more
—always less
—constantly inconstant
And you and I?
We are stones!
Not just builders
but also the built.
Not just destroyers,
but also the destroyed.
Temptor and tempted
playing the personae
in the drama
of temptations,
we exist
most of the time
in the wilderness,
the place of stones' confusion.
Not so much from nature
as from second nature,
we lean first one way
and then another
teetering
from more to less
and back again.

Our stoney temptations
want to keep us
from being
who we are,
whose we are,
and who
we might be.
The monuments,
temples,
and prisons
find expression
in our lives,
and our dust and ashes
wait patiently
to be born
of demise.
Yet promise
holds the hand
of threat.
Only in the
wilderness of our lives—
the place of
stoney temptations—
only here
can we explore
limit and possibility.
Only in the wilderness
can our hunger
be assuaged
through fasting,
Only here
can we come
to know
stones
and
ourselves. ☦

Symbols Of Holy Week

by Elaine M. Ward

A symbol not only represents, but has its own meaning, energy or message. We look at a traffic sign and it is simply a sign to STOP or GO, but when we look at a symbol we enter it. We participate in its message because it is charged with emotions, and we bring our emotions, our head and heart, to it.

In the church our task is to keep alive the symbol so that it remains fresh and relevant to the hearer/seer. When the church or any hearer cuts itself off from symbol, Christianity becomes empty conformity, obedience without imagination. It is not an easy job to prevent creeds from becoming codified, religious instincts from becoming institutionalized, and sacred stories from becoming conventional morality, written dogma or doctrine, thus removing the authentic, dynamic religious element in them. Symbols are the subjective encounter and dialogue with God.

Symbols help us see, for they represent realities that point beyond themselves. The meaning and purpose of religion for Christianity and Judaism lie in the relationship of the individual to God, experienced symbolically. We are surrounded by the symbols of the faith in the church: the cross, altar, candles, Bible, baptismal font, Holy Communion. We have both visual and verbal symbols.

Symbols are outward signs of inward realities, of deeper truths, and as long as they are channels that lead to the transcendent God, they are life-giving and life-preserving.

Lent is a season of symbols. The following symbols represent the season of Lent. Participate in them with the following activities.

Palm Branch

On Palm Sunday the palm branches remind us of the procession of Jesus riding on an unbroken colt into the city, while the people spread their cloaks on the way and cried, "Hosanna! Alleluia!"

Read Matthew 21:1-11; Mark 11:1-10; Luke 19:28-40; John 12:12-19.

Money Bag

On the second day of Holy Week we read of Jesus overturning the tables of the money changers. Money bags are the symbols of those who sold sacrificial offerings, of Judas who betrayed his master for 30 coins of silver, for priests selling penances, and still today, for those whose money is their idol in place of God.

Make a list of how you spend your money.

Face with Eyes Crying

On the third day Jesus wept over Jerusalem and their political and religious system. We cannot help but wonder where Jesus is weeping today. I have chosen the symbol of tears for this day. Lent is a time of weeping. In this time and in this place we cry our prayers to God, who collects our tears.

Write a prayer of intercession.

Knife

Wednesday was the day of betrayal. Judas made a bargain with the religious leaders to turn Jesus over to them. Judas is a symbol of our cutting off commitment to Christ for other priorities in our life.

Reflect on and discuss with a partner or in a small group your greatest fear.

Chalice

The chalice represents Maundy Thursday. Maundy means commandment, reminding us of Jesus' commandment to love one another (John 13:34). On the fifth day of Holy Week Jesus celebrated Passover with his disciples. They ate together and Jesus took the cup and told us to remember him whenever we eat and drink together, especially in the celebration of Holy Communion.

Have a communion service or share a snack together, remembering Jesus.

Cross

On the sixth day Jesus was crucified. The cross represents Good Friday when God took our symbol of cruelty and torture and transformed it into a symbol of God's love. Good Friday means "God's Friday."

It is a symbol of forgiveness, as Jesus said on the cross, "Father, forgive them for they know not what they do."

We say, "Forgive us our trespasses, as we forgive..." The failure to forgive is to place a tourniquet on God's mercy and love, for with God all things are possible!

Pray a prayer of confession and words of assurance.

Tomb

On the seventh day the body of Jesus was placed in a borrowed tomb. It is the day of passage. Baptism in the early church took place on this day. The tomb is the symbol of dying with Christ to be reborn in the waters of baptism.

Discuss with a partner: What is the Good Friday in your life?

?

Easter is the eighth day, the first day of this new week, the day of resurrection. What symbol would you give to this holy day?

Egg

Christians are known as Easter people and eggs are a symbol of new "beginning," holding new life within its shell. At Easter Christians celebrate by giving and receiving eggs, a symbol of new life and their roundness a symbol of eternal life. Christians paint crosses on eggs to remember Christ's death and resurrection. The shell of the egg can also represent the tomb from which Christ emerged on Easter morning.

Projects:

1. Dye Easter eggs not only for the joy of the smell (the aroma of vinegar will be an eternal reminder of a tradition that combines sight, smell, taste, touch and sound [crack eggs together before you eat them]), but for the joy of what they represent. Talk about the egg as a symbol of new life, new being, because of Jesus' death and resurrection. Jesus' body was wrapped in linens and placed in a tomb, as the new life of a baby chick is "entombed" in a shell and comes out a living creature. Egg rolling is symbolic of the rolling away of the stone on Easter. What a miracle is God's plan for life! What a miracle is God's plan for new life "in Christ"!

2. Choose an egg of your choice and decorate it with symbols of Easter. Other symbols include: lilies—white is the color of purity, joy, and light; the bulb—the tomb of Jesus, the blossom for life after death; the palm leaf—carried by Jesus' people rejoicing on Palm Sunday; nails—symbols of Jesus' suffering, "I.N.R.I": Jesus of Nazarenus, Rex Judaeorum, King of the Jews; crown of thorns— mockery crown placed on Jesus' head; chalice or grail—cup of wine Jesus blessed at the Last Supper; bread—Jesus as the bread of life, one of the elements of the Holy Communion.

3. Think and talk about Easter customs in other parts of the world, such as in Bulgaria where the first dyed egg is placed in front of an "icon" (picture of Christ) in the kitchen beside a lighted candle. ✟

Section Two
Children

A Lenten Learning Center

by Peter Olsen

Children learn at their best when they can participate in the learning activity. Learning centers allow for hands-on learning. Religious education is most effective when there is participation, not just observation.

Our Lenten Learning Center was designed to achieve three purposes:
- Give a visual focus for learning the stories of Lent.
- Excite the children's imagination and curiosity.
- Allow for the biblical message to penetrate more meaningful through a multimedia approach that personally involves each student.

Sounds like a tough assignment, but it turns out to be easier than expected and exceptionally effective.

We chose to focus on four events or concepts related to the Lent experience, the raising of Lazarus (John 11:1-44), the Last Supper (Luke 22:14-23), entering into Jerusalem (Luke 19:28-38), and the resurrection (Matthew 28:1-10). Each event was to be shared with students as it is related in scripture but with an added emphasis that comes with a hands-on experience. We hoped that "visualization" and a certain amount of participation would reinforce the learning experience.

We began with planning. One person would be in charge of planning and leading each of the four learning centers. A simple auditorium or large room is sufficient for the program. Each of the four corners can be the location of one center. An alternative, if too much noise or distracting is anticipated, is to use four different classrooms.

Classes would be divided into four groups. We choose K-1, 2-3, 4-5, and 6-8 as the groups. At the beginning of the hour, each group would start at one of the four learning centers (corners of the room) and change centers every 15-20 minutes. In this fashion, each group had a chance to work at each learning center during the church school hour.

THE FOUR CENTERS

THE RAISING OF LAZARUS

Collect appropriate costumes for the players, for Jesus and Lazarus and one or two helpers. Find a bench or use three chairs as the "grave" for Lazarus. Choose one student to be wrapped in newspapers to simulate Lazarus. Lay that person on the bench and as the story of the Lazarus is told, have students "raise" him, unwrap his grave cloths, and declare him living again. The leader is the storyteller and as the story is told, even the youngest student can role-play the action. Focus for the leader is that anything can happen with God, even the possibility of new life.

THE LAST SUPPER

Set up tables and chairs, enough for the whole group, to simulate the setting of the Last Supper. Have name tags of each of the disciples placed on the table in front of the chairs. If there are fewer or more than twelve, have students share roles. Prepare cups to be used for the grape juice and small slices of bread.

Begin by relating information about each of the disciples at the table with Jesus for the Passover meal. Students assume the role of that disciple with help from the leader. As the teacher relates the biblical story of the Last Supper, the bread and grape jucie can be shared with students and the scriptual words of Jesus shared. Emphasis for the leader needs to focus on how Jesus shared his ministry with his friends, informed them who he was, and what his purpose was. It is important that the leader does not recreate the eucharists, but rather informs students of the biblical background as forerunner for what the regular communion service celebrates.

Word Find

by Ann Bateman

Find the names of 14 symbols which remind us of the stories of Jesus at the time of the Last Supper, Crucifixion and Resurrection.

- BASIN
- BULB
- CHALICE
- CROWN OF THORNS
- EGG
- MONEY BAG
- PHOENIX
- BREAD
- BUTTERFLY
- CROSS
- DICE
- EMPTY TOMB
- NAIL
- TOWEL

```
T O W E L O S R A H E N B R
L M T Y N G N O N O I X E R
E P T N O G R W I A D T O S
W O X I N E O H P W E L C O
G O M S F T H I Y A G G B S
G A B A H O T L I A N L M E
E A B B R N F D L I E M O P
B A B Y C R O S S C E T T Y
G U L Y E E N T O R F N Y O
B B A T E N W M B W H S T E
L E T I C N O C O N R M P Y
U U S N I X R M O T O N M B
B R E A D Y C H A L I C E A
```

PALM SUNDAY

The Palm Sunday celebration recreates Jesus' entry into the city of Jerusalem. Having a donkey present is the visual focus for children. Create one using a piano bench or something similiar. To the bench attach a cardboard head, some ears, a tail, and four legs. That ought to be sufficient to incite some imagination. Have rolls of newspaper prepared so that each child can cut the folds and pull out a make believe palm branch. Directions for making paper fold palm branches are readily available in arts and crafts books.

As the leader recreates the biblical story, children can take turns riding the donkey and waving palm branches. Again, this is a hands-on experience, a simulation to help children focus on and remember the biblical event.

THE RESURRECTION

Have a wooden cross, hand made from some poles, placed in the center of a circle of chairs, enough for each student. Either make or purchase (Cokesbury) small, colorful paper crosses, enough for each student. As students arrive at this center, pass out the crosses. This center is the place to focus on the Easter event. Dialogue with the students is most helpful here. Invite the minister or other theological astute teacher to share with students the many meanings of the cross in the life of the Christian. Ask students to share what the cross symbolizes for them. Sing and pray together as a concluding experience for this center.

It is important to remember in planning that different ages groups will be at each center throughout the church school hour. Leaders need to prepare to speak in a language appropriate for each age group, to recruit other teachers to help students do the hands-on activities, and not, I repeat, not expect deep theological understanding from the students. The purpose of the centers is to help students put together the various episodes In Jesus's life during those last few days. The interpretation and deeper theological reflection belongs at a later time in their faith journey. ✞

Lent: A Time For Listening

by Joanne Wilson

OBJECTIVE: To teach ways God speaks to us and the importance of listening and obeying.

BACKGROUND SCRIPTURE: Matthew 7:24-27; James 1:22.

MEMORY VERSE: Matthew 11:15

THEME INTRODUCTION

Before the meeting, make a tape recording of sounds familiar to your students, including sounds from a church service. Or ask students to give sounds behind a sheet, such as, a bell, a whistle, dropping a spoon, etc.

Distribute paper and pencils. Encourage the students to write the sound on the paper. Pause between sounds to give time for thought. When finished, repeat the sounds and give the answers.

Stress listening skills with the following questions:
- Have you ever been daydreaming when your teacher was talking? Explain.
- Why is it important to listen at home and in school?
- Why is it important to listen to God?
- Why is the Lenten season a good time to emphasize listening skills?

EXPLORATION ACTIVITIES

Before class write the following on a chalkboard: The Lenten season is a special time to listen to God. How did God speak in Bible times? How does God speak to me today?

Divide the class into groups of three or four. Give each group one of the following references. (Answers in parentheses for the leader.)

I Kings 17:16 (directly)
Exodus 3:26 (burning bush)
Luke 2:8-12 (angels)
Genesis 28:10-15 (dream)
Acts 8:26-28, 34-35 (God spoke to Philip through an angel. He spoke to the Ethiopian man through Philip.)

Reassemble the groups to report discoveries.

INDIVIDUAL CREATIVITY

Distribute paper and markers. Ask student to illustrate ways God speaks today, in picture or poster form. Suggestions: God speaks through parents, teachers, pastors, prayer, music, worship, Sunday school lesson, reading, friends, television, radio, etc.

Ask each student to show and explain their picture. Add answers above that were not mentioned by the students.

BIBLE DRILL

One way God speaks to us today is through the Bible. Seat the students in a row. Write one Bible reference on the chalkboard at a time. The first student to find it, stands, and reads the verse. After the verse is discussed, the student goes to the head of the line while others move down giving him/her the first seat. Students on the first and second seat are disqualified from looking up the next verse. The student at the head of the line at the end of the game is the winner. Use as many references as time permits.

Release Butterflies

by Delia Halverson

Adults, as well as children, enjoy releasing butterflies. Caterpillars may be ordered by calling 1-800-LIVE BUG. They will be shipped to you with instructions for just when to begin feeding them a specific food so they come out of the chrysalis just when you want to release them.

Place the caterpillars at a place where the whole church can enjoy watching the process. At the appointed time, say a prayer for the butterflies before releasing them outside. Wear bright colored clothing, and the butterflies will probably linger around and even light on your shoulder. ✟

I Peter 1:25
Romans 15:4
Matthew 4:4
I John 5:13
Psalm 119:9
Psalm 12:6,7
John 20:31
Proverbs 287

BIBLE GAME

Pin familiar Bible names on the back of each student and seat them in a circle. A student stands in the center, asking questions to help him/her guess the name on his/her back. When a person guesses correctly, he/she chooses another person. Conclude by emphasizing that God spoke to people in Bible times. God speaks to us today. We must listen.

BIBLE ACTIVITY

Read James 1:22 and discuss. Make a copy of the following activity for each student.

HEARERS AND DOERS

Write one of these names on each line: Moses, Jonah, Noah, Ananias, Pharaoh, Eve, Abraham. The Bible verses will help you.

"Go into the street called Straight." (Acts 9:10-11)
_____

"Make an ark of gopher wood." (Genesis 6:13-14)
_____

"Bring my people out of Egypt." (Exodus 3:10-11)
_____

"Go up the mountain and offer your son." (Genesis 22:2-3)
_____

HEARERS ONLY

"Go to Ninevah." (Jonah 1:1-2)
_____

"Let my people go." (Exodus 5:12)
_____

"Don't eat the fruit of this tree." (Genesis 2:17, 3:6)
_____

CONCLUSION: Guide the group in formulating answers to the following questions: What should I know as a result of this lesson? How should I feel as a result of this lesson? What should I do in response to this lesson?

CLOSING PRAYER: Dear God, help us listen for Your voice. Help us obey and live for God every day. In Jesus name. Amen. ✟

Lenten Symbols Banner

by Carolyn Egolf

Discuss the following symbols with children and explain their importance to Lent. Then have the children draw the symbols and cut them out of felt and assemble for a banner.

1. Palms—The crowd waved palms to celebrate Jesus' coming to Jerusalem. That's why we call Sunday before Easter Palm Sunday.

2. Bread & Cup—The bread symbolizes Jesus' body, and the cup represents his blood. We call this Holy Communion or the Last Supper. Jesus gave new meaning to unleavened bread and wine used by the Jews to celebrate Passover.

3. Towel & Basin—Jesus washed the disciples' feet to show them humility and service. He reminded them that "If any one would be first, he must be last of all and servant of all." (Mark 9:35b)

4. Cross—Jesus was crucified on a cross. We use many forms of an empty cross to symbolize Christ's death and resurrection. The cross reminds us how much God really does love us.

5. Nails—Nails symbolize Jesus' suffering as he hung on the cross.

6. Butterfly—Because it changes in form, the butterfly is a symbol of new life. We are promised new life in Christ.

7. Crown—Jesus wore a crown of thorns. Soldiers made this to mock him. We are promised "an unfading crown of glory." (I Pet. 5:4b)

8. Vine—Jesus spoke of himself as the Vine, and we are the branches. If we abide with him, stay close to him, He will give us courage and strength to live for him.

All these things remind us of what Easter means and why it is the holiest day in the Christian year.

Scripture quotations are from Holy Bible—Revised Standard Version. Thomas Nelson & Sons, Camden, N.J. 1952.

New Life

by Jane Maehr

New life may or may not be a concept that is readily understood by young children. It may have meaning for the child who has an infant sibling or it may have the almost magical meaning that modern children make of "morphing" on television cartoons! But, to bring a spiritual dimension to a life science experience, and bring joy and "new life" to adults as well as children, here's an interpretation of a frequently used Lenten symbol—bulbs.

Early in Lent

Teachers of elementary age children will have informal conversations with children about the symbolism of Lent and Easter. Together they will explore the misunderstandings, the treachery, the despair, that led to crucifixion and, finally, to the exultation. What had been lost, what had been destroyed, what had been mourned was surprisingly reversed. It was surprisingly reconstructed. Death became Life!

Teachers will easily move to using analogies, e.g., "It's a lot like a common bulb that might be planted in your garden." Elicit from children comments about the bulb's appearance..."It's brown and dry," "It looks dead," "It looks yucky!" Add accurate information at an appropriate developmental level about bulbs, e.g., while appearing lifeless, this bulb has the capacity to become a plant; bulbs are a form of a seed; the germ of a new plant is within this bulb, together with a supply of food which will sustain the bulb; from this small lifeless appearing sphere, a new living plant can arise, thrive, and bring joy; if such a bulb is planted in our yard, while appearing to be dead, it changes while waiting in the soil, and brings forth new life. This is now a plant that lives where earlier it had appeared hopelessly lifeless.

A Month Before Easter

Teachers will collect: plastic margarine tubs; pea gravel or small stones; paper white narcissus bulbs.

As an outgrowth of the discussions about bulbs as a symbol of "new life", invite children to prepare a plastic container with their name and add a shallow layer of gravel or stones. Help children position one narcissus bulb (root end down) on the stones and continue filling the container with gravel and stones, leaving at least 1/4 of the bulb uncovered. Add water—enough to thoroughly moisten the stones but not so much that the bulb itself is totally immersed in water. Leave the bulbs in the classroom until the next week—with the possibility that the custodian or church secretary just might look in on them! (Teachers should plant several extras for new students, bulbs that may not grow, ones that get dropped, etc.)

Each of the Next Sundays

Each Sunday, check on the nearly miraculous happenings—a sprout will become a shoot; the stem and leaves will grow rapidly and buds will form! Exult with the children over each happening and manipulate the light conditions—more sun, less sun, turned, etc. to gauge the speed with which the project moves on. Speculate on what the next stage will be and evaluate the growing conditions.

On Easter

There are few blooming plants more spectacular than blooming narcissus bulbs and these bulbs will bring joy to all who behold them! They may be grouped in a display in the sanctuary or narthex; they may be centerpieces for the congregation's Easter breakfast; they may add fragrance to the entire educational portion of the church! The bulbs may be taken home to extend the celebration of the Feast of the Resurrection—the Time of New Life—and shared with friends in nursing homes or hospitals.

Teachers may choose to recycle the margarine tubs and rocks for another year.

Enjoy a symbol of God's strength at its most fragrant and most beautiful!

A note: The effect of this project was spectacular! Several years ago, I organized this with the entire Church School at Bethlehem United Church of Christ in Ann Arbor, MI. Nearly 150 blooming narcissus bulbs centered the Easter breakfast tables and young and old were thrilled. ✛

All God's Children

by Jane Maehr

The Gospel message emphasizes a universal quality. Christ was born, a gift for all. Christ suffered and died, a substitute for all. Christ conquered death, guaranteeing New Life for all. Nonetheless, ours is a world where too often communities and opportunities are not open to all, where ethnic and racial suspicion and competition all too often *exclude* rather than *include*. It is helpful to plan an activity that celebrates diversity while recognizing the underlying fact of being a part of one family—the family of God.

- Plan ahead to make "All God's Children Cookies", using a basic stir-and-drop sugar cookie recipe such as Stir-n-Drop Sugar Cookies or another sugar cookie or a ginger cookie recipe for cutouts. If possible, involve the students in bringing the ingredients. A surprisingly large number of children no longer know the fun of making cookies "from scratch," so plan to spend plenty of time talking about the ingredients, where they come from, and what effect these ingredients have on the cookies.

Stir-n-Drop Sugar Cookies

3 egg whites
3/4 cup sugar
2/3 cup vegetable oil
2 cups flour
2 tsp. vanilla
2 tsp. baking power
1 tsp. grated lemon rind
1/2 tsp. salt

Heat oven to 400; beat egg whites with fork. Stir in oil, vanilla, lemon. Blend in sugar until mixture thickens. Measure flour and stir together with baking powder and salt; blend in. Drop dough by teaspoonfuls about 2" apart on ungreased baking sheet. Flatten with oiled bottom of glass dipped in sugar. Bake 8 to 10 min. Makes about 4 dozen 2-1/2" cookies.

- After everyone has helped mix the basic cookie recipe, set aside a portion of the dough to leave plain. Explain that today's cookies are going to represent the wonderful varieties of God's children—the cookies will be *diverse,* i.e., they will have many variations while remaining basically alike because they started from the same recipe, using the same ingredients. Some cookies will be light colored, some dark colored, some cookies will have different flavors—yet all cookies will be delicious!
- Divide the remaining dough into several portions and get ready to use your imagination! Add any of these or other ingredients to each of the portions:
    *chocolate chips, M & M's, peanut butter pieces, butterscotch pieces
    coconut or cinnamon red hot candies
    chopped pecans, walnuts, or salted peanuts
    sunflower or pumpkin seeds
    cocoa
    food coloring
    dried cherries, dried apricots or raisin oatmeal*

- Continue the discussion about the possibilities of how interesting these variations of sugar cookies are likely to be…some have color, some crunch, some chewiness, some sweetness, etc. Before baking, even consider adding incredible concluding touches such as colored sugar, cinnamon/sugar, candy sprinkles etc.

- While the cookies are baking, prepare the room for a "God's Love For All" snack time:
    Position a globe or map, together with the Bible, near where the snack will be served. Choose an appropriate portion of Scripture to read as part of the devotion. Pour white and chocolate milk or offer several kinds of fruit juice. Play taped or recorded music from several countries. Consider having some serving pieces that represent different places

Waxed Onions

by Delia Halverson

Better than Easter eggs, waxed sprouted onions last up to six weeks and symbolize new birth from something that appears dead.

Locate onions that are beginning to sprout. Bring water to boil in an electric fry pan. Place an empty vegetable can in the water and put old candles or paraffin and crayons (of the desired color) in the can. Keep the water simmering and allow the candles and crayons to melt. Cans of additional colors may be added. Use craft sticks to stir the wax periodically, distributing the color. (Food color will not work because it must mix with water.)

When the wax has melted, grasp an onion by the sprout and dip it into the wax quickly, allowing the wax to come only to the base of the sprout. Repeat the procedure several times, allowing it to cool in between dips. After cooling the onions may be decorated with dribbles of melted wax of varying colors.

Place the waxed onions in a basket with Easter grass and keep them out of direct sun and away from any heat source. The sprouts will continue to grow, symbolizing Christ's new life from the dead. ✞

---

in the world, e.g., a woven basket, a clay pot, a carved bowl.

Invite guests who might wear an item of clothing from another country, e.g., a serape, an Australian hat, a dirndl from Germany, a woven garment from Africa, a leaf hat from southeast Asia. Invite someone who might be able to offer phrases in Spanish, Vietnamese, French etc.

- When the cookies are baked and cooled, it's time to celebrate! Join hands in a circle, using a prayer such as this one:

    God of all people, we remember that we are all Your children. You have created us with varied interest and beauty. You have placed us around the world in different climates and provided us with varied foods to eat. You have given us varied gifts and talents. You have helped us speak different words and sing different songs. God, we remember, too, that You suffered for each of us, You died for each of us, You secured Easter for each of us. God of all people, help us to love each other—we are all part of Your family. Help us to live together in peace. We celebrate! Amen.

- As the party progresses, use the opportunity to identify countries around the world while finding places on the globe. Most importantly, enjoy eating "cookie diversity" while enjoying discussing the gift of diversity from a God who wisely chose to make the world's people as interesting and as varied as these cookies! ✞

A Walk Through Holy Week

by Penny Lowes

Invite the entire congregation to experience the final week of Christ's life in the multi-media presentation of A Walk Through Holy Week. This "walk" is a special church school presentation prepared, and presented by, the children in their respective church school classes. Traditionally taking place on Palm Sunday, this event is sure to become an integral part of your Lenten season. If Palm Sunday is not convenient, the Holy Walk could be presented on any Sunday during the season of Lent.

The following directions will explain how to establish the walk in the church school. This event could also be adapted to an intergenerational, all church format.

The events of Holy Week, from Palm Sunday to Easter, are depicted in diorama form. The possibilities are limitless. Each class or group must create and present a display that in some way depicts the occurrences on the historical day for which they are assigned. Scenes range from living dioramas to eggshell mosaics. The scenes are presented in a large open area—such as a fellowship hall or gymnasium. Each class is assigned an area in which to display their scene. These areas are situated in the chronological order of the week's events.

Following the Palm Sunday worship service, parishioners are invited to "stroll" through Holy Week. Signs are posted to direct traffic. Students are required to stand near their diorama to answer questions and explain the process and events depicted. Hot cross buns, coffee, tea, and juice may be provided as refreshments. (Recipe for Hot Cross Buns follows.)

Preparation and Planning

Set the Date. Meet with your church council and minister to set the date for the walk through. Choose a time that will be convenient and accessible for the teachers, students and entire viewing congregation.

Establish the Location. Choose a large room or area where the walk will take place. We used eight-foot tables to define each space. If you are in a warm climate, you may want to consider an outdoor location.

The walk could be easily adapted to an entire church setting. Perhaps the students would create the scenes in their meeting place, and the congregants would stroll through the church school. Or, you may have a large narthex or entry area where members could view the scenes on the way into worship. Whatever the location, be sure that it can accommodate the traffic and suit the needs of all (i.e. be handicap accessible).

Determine The Theme Days From Holy: Week These are the days that you will be covering during the walk through. Select appropriate scripture references to accompany the themes. When possible, give more than one scripture reference. There are many possible days and events that may be depicted. Pick the ones that are well-suited for your groups' ability and understanding. For example, preschoolers love the donkey ride into Jerusalem and the waving of palm branches. The crucifixion of Jesus is more appropriate for the middle school or high school ages. Possible topics include:

- *Palm Sunday:* Matthew 21:1-11; Mark 11:1-11; Luke 19:28-40; John 12:12-19.
- *Jesus in the Temple:* Matthew 21:12-17; Mark 11:15-19; Luke 19:45-48; John 2:13-22.
- *The Plot Against Jesus:* Matthew 26:1-5; Mark 14:1-2; Luke 22:1-2; John 11:45-53.
- *Jesus is Anointed at Bethany:* Matthew 26:6-13; Mark 14:3-9; John 12:1-9.
- *Judas Agrees to Betray Jesus:* Matthew 26:14-16; Mark 14:10-11; Luke 22:36.
- *The Passover Meal and Last Supper:* Matthew 26:17-30; Mark 14:12-26; Luke 22:7-23; John 13:21-30; I Corinthians 11:23-25.
- *Jesus Prays in Gethsemane:* Matthew 26:36-44; Mark 14:32-42; Luke 22:39-46.
- *The Arrest of Jesus:* Matthew 26:47-56; Mark 14:43-50; Luke 22:47-53; John 18:3-12.
- *Peter Denies Jesus:* Matthew 26:69-75; Mark 14:66-72; Luke 22:56-62; John 18:15-18, 25-27.
- *Jesus is Crucified:* Matthew 27:32-55; Mark

14:21-41; Luke 23:13-43; John 19:1-27.
- **The Burial of Jesus:** Matthew 27:57-66; Mark 15:42-43; Luke 23:50-56; John 19:38-42.
- **The Empty Tomb and Jesus Appears to Mary Magdelene:** Matthew 28:1-15; John 20:1-18; Luke 24:1-12; Mark 16:1-11.

Other topics may be chosen, such as, the Great Commandment, and the parables that Jesus told while in Jerusalem. You will need to decide how many scenes you can realistically display, and which will best relay the message that you wish to impart.

Meet with the Teachers: The teachers must have a clear understanding of the project and ample preparation time. It is suggested that the teachers be included in the planning from the beginning of Lent on Ash Wednesday. The amount of preparation time is influenced by the age of the students, the difficulty of the theme, and the kind of display that the class elects to portray.

Assign the Topic: Topics may be assigned or you may let the teachers choose their respective events. The topics can be assigned by individual grade level, or two groups might work together. If you have an adult church school, they might also be given a holy week topic.

Let the Creative Work Begin! Encourage the teachers to brainstorm with their classes about how to best portray their assigned day. You will be amazed at the ideas that pour forth. Even if the teachers are not experienced in art or drama, the students often are! Here are some ideas:

- Students act out the scene in costumes, with backdrop, etc.
- Make mosaic pictures of event using eggshells, cut paper, tiles, etc.
- Create collages with pictures from magazines, drawings, coloring, etc.
- Make model figures using clay, clothespins, pipe cleaners, dolls, etc.
- Life-size tracing of students are cut out, painted and dressed to be biblical figures.
- Film a video recording of the class acting out the scene.
- Try a copper punch relief, wood burning, or woodcarvings.
- Draw a large mural on cloth or paper.
- Create a cartoon comic strip of the event on large paper.
- Have a puppet show.
- Assemble papier mache figures.
- Have live animals (for the brave) to help create the desired atmosphere.

The possibilities are endless!

Publicize the "Walk Through Holy Week." Be sure that everyone in the church is informed about this exciting and educational event. Publish announcements in the church newsletter and during worship services leading up to Palm Sunday. Put up posters and send home notes with the students telling parents about the event.

Schedule a Set-up Period for the Classes. Allow ample time for setup so that the presentations are ready before the parishioners appear.

Congratulations You are now ready to enjoy a moving and educational celebration of the final days in the life of our Lord, Jesus Christ. All who participate will find their faith strengthened and enhanced through the creative efforts of the church school. May the powerful love and beautiful truth of the resurrection be experienced by all.

Sample "Walk Through Holy Week"

Preschool (3's and 4's): Palm Sunday

This group made large green palms from construction paper. Children took turns riding on the colt (a rocking horse) while the other class members chanted "Hosannah" and sang "Ho-Ho-Ho Hosannah."

Four-year-olds and Kindergarten: Jesus In the Temple

These students drew a large mural of a temple. They dressed as money-changers and peddlers and pantomimed Jesus overturning the tables with goods and coins scattered about. They stood in statue formation with surprised and angry looks frozen on their faces. A few other students explained what had happened.

First and Second Graders: The Passover Meal and Lord's Supper

In their own words students paraphrased and wrote

out the story from scriptures on large pieces of poster board that were used as the backdrop. In front of the posters they set a table with a bright colored cloth, a goblet of wine, and a plate of bread that they had kneaded and baked.

Third Graders: Jesus Prays in Gethsemane

This group took two large overcoat boxes, lined them with plastic trash bags, filled them with potting soil and planted grass. After the grass had sprouted, they put in rocks, twig trees, and figures made from clothespins and cloth scraps. (The grass got so long before the walk through that it had to be "mowed" with scissors!)

Fourth Graders: The Arrest of Jesus

This class made three-foot tall figures from tag board. The faces were painted, yarn and fabric were added for the clothes and hair. Aluminum foil swords and armor protected the soldiers. The figures were mounted on dowels, and the students kneeled behind a cloth draped table to present the scene in puppet-show style.

Fifth and Sixth Graders: The Burial of Jesus

Individual shoebox dioramas were made and displayed to show various depictions of Jesus wrapped in cloth and lying in the tomb guarded by a soldier. Some showed an angel visiting him.

Seventh and Eighth Graders: Jesus is Crucified

A large papier mache Golgotha was created. Three stick crosses were mounted on the hill and the words to scripture were printed on a plaque.

Senior High Students: The Tomb is Empty

A script was written, parts learned and this group acted out and recorded their scene on video. They used modern day language, clothing, and setting to share their topic. The video was shown non-stop throughout the walk through while the students answered questions about their topic.

Additional Suggestions:

The educational value of the "Walk Through Holy Week" can be further enhanced through the use of a questionnaire. Each class should prepare three questions whose answers may be found at their respective displays. The questions can then be scrambled and compiled in one list. As the congregants, and students, stroll through Holy Week, they find the answers and write them on their sheet. This activity will provide greater meaning as the participants actively seek to find the answers and, consequently, learn more about what is happening at each display. A sample questionnaire follows.

A Holy Week Questionnaire:

1) Peter was very upset when he heard the cock crow. Why?
2) What is the name of the hill where Christ was crucified? How did it get this name?
3) How much money was Judas paid to betray Christ?
4) What is a money-changer? Why was Christ angry with the money-changers in the temple?
5) What is Gethsemane? What happened there?
6) Who said, "Hosannah?" Why? What does it mean?
7) How did Jesus come back into Jerusalem?
8) What is the Last Supper? What did Jesus say about the bread? About the wine?
9) Who were the women that went to the tomb?
10) How was Jesus buried?

Recipe for Hot Cross Buns:
    4 cups flour
    2 packages dry yeast
    3/4 t. ground cinnamon
    3/4 cup milk
    1/3 cup sugar
    1/2 cup vegetable oil
    3/4 t. salt
    3 eggs
    2/3 cup currants
    1 egg white slightly beaten

Combine 2 cups of the flour, the yeast and cinnamon. Mix well. Scald milk, then stir in the sugar, oil and salt. Let the mixture cool to lukewarm. Gradually add the milk mixture to the flour mixture, beating at low speed with an electric mixer. Add the 3 eggs and beat for 3 minutes at high speed. Stir in the currants and enough remaining flour to make a soft dough. Knead 5 minutes. Place in a well greased bowl and turn over so that the top is greased. Cover and let rise in a warm place for about 1-1/2 hours, or until doubled in bulk. Punch down, cover and let rest for 10 minutes. Divide the dough into 18 pieces (large buns) or 36 pieces (small buns). Shape into balls and place 2 inches (large) or 1 inch (small) apart on a greased cookie sheet. Cover and let rise in a warm place (85 degrees) for 1 hour until doubled in bulk. Using a sharp knife, cut a shallow cross on top of each bun. Brush with egg white. Bake at 375 degrees 10-12 minutes. Cool on wire rack.

Icing:
    1 cup powdered sugar
    1 tablespoon milk
    1/2 teaspoon vanilla extract

Combine the powdered sugar, milk and vanilla. Mix well and pipe into indentations on each bun. Yield: 1-1/2 dozen large buns or 3 dozen small buns. ✞

Lenten Puzzler

by Ellen Humbert

How much do you know about Lent? Test yourself with this Lenten Puzzler. Read each clue and fill in the numbered squares with your answers.

1. __(8)__ days before Easter, not counting Sundays, there begins the religious season of Lent.

2. Lent means lengthening __(6)__.

3. The first day of this season is Ash __(3)__

4. The days of Lent recall the same number of days that Jesus spent in the __(12)__.

5. During this time, He fasted and became strong as He prepared for his work in the __(5)__.

6. Many Christians today look for ways during this time to become better and stronger, to make a fresh __(14)__.

7. As a symbol of this change in themselves, they may __(15)__ up certain pleasures or try to break bad habits during Lent.

8. The last week of Lent is called __(16)__ Week.

9. __(7)__ Sunday is the first day of this last week.

10. In many Christian churches, everyone goes home with a __(13)__ from the tree after which this Sunday is named.

11. This reminds us that these (#10) were spread before Jesus when he rode into __(2)__.

12. He had come there with his disciples to celebrate __(1)__, the Hebrew festival of freedom.

13. The fifth day of the last week in Lent is called __(11)__ Thursday.

14. This day is set aside to honor the Lord's __(10)__, or Holy Communion.

15. Good Friday is a day of __(9)__, which is set aside for remembering Jesus' death.

16. Easter Eve, or Holy __(4)__, is the day before Easter. Sometime during this day or evening, mourning for Jesus stops and joyful celebrations begin. ✝

(The answer to the puzzle is on page 110)

He Has Risen!

by Joyce DeToni-Hill

This text is based upon Luke 24: 19

Children love to act out the Easter resurrection story. This dramatic call to worship is adaptable for a variety of ages and number of participants. It sets a joyful tone for any worship service in Easter or Eastertide.

Participants: 1 or 2 angels; 1 woman; 2 or more disciples scattered about the sanctuary; 1 person "planted" in the congregation; 1 narrator.

Props: costumes if desired; spices.

Prepare: Before narrator begins, disciples are scattered about the sanctuary, the women are off to the side, angels are behind communion table or hidden somewhere else on chancel.

Narrator: On the first day of the week, very early in the morning, the women took spices they had prepared and went to the tomb. *(Women walk slowly and sadly to the chancel)*

Narrator: But when they entered, they did not find the body of the Lord Jesus. *(Women look around the "tomb" area carefully, acting puzzled.)*

Narrator: While they were wondering about this, suddenly two angels in clothes that gleamed like lightening stood beside them. *(Angels come out of hiding and stand in front of the women.)*

Narrator: In their fright the women bowed down with their faces to the ground. *(Women step back quickly in surprise and drop their spices. They bow down before the angels)*

Narrator: But the angel said to them," Why do you look for the living among the dead? He is not here; he has risen! Remember how he told you, while he was still in Galilee: The Son of Man must be delivered into the hands of sinful people, be crucified, and on the third day be raised again." *(While narrator speaks the angel(s) may pantomime the the words or an angel may speak the words instead of the narrator)*

Narrator: Then they remembered his words. *(Women rise and shake their heads. Yes, they had remembered!)*

Narrator: They ran from the tomb and told all these things to the Eleven and all the others. *(The women then "run" to the first disciple standing in the sanctuary. A designated Mary Magdaline exclaims to the disciple:*

"Have you heard?" The disciple says NO! The women huddle as if to whisper an exciting message. No one is to hear the message but the disciple. Upon hearing the message the disciple exclaims an assigned response such as, "Isn't that wonderful?", "Is that right?", "Alleluia!", "Praise God," "Horray!", etc. Younger children seem to respond best with a preassigned response.

The entire group "runs" to the next disciple and the scene is repeated until all the disciples have been told. As the last of the disciples is told this exciting secret message, they all gather back on the steps of the chancel. As they do, the "plant" from the congregation stands up and announces loudly, "Hey, what's all this excitement about?" The entire group responds together, "Have you not heard? He has risen! Alleluia!"✝

Easter Lilies

by Linda Bloomgren

It is easy for children to understand why the Easter lily is a symbol of Easter. From a dry and lifeless-looking lily bulb, the lily plant grows and blossoms with new life. We are reminded of the new life that is ours through Jesus' resurrection.

During Lent, your students can make Easter lilies to celebrate the new life of Easter. Have each child cut a white paper plate in half. Roll one of the plate halves into a cone shape and fasten it with clear tape. Cut the remaining plate half into four pie-shaped wedges. These will be the lily petals. Tape the lily petals around the pointed base of the cone.

To make the stem, push a green pipe cleaner through the flower's cone-shaped center. Let part of the green stem show inside the flower to form a stamen. Cut a small oval shape from yellow construction paper and glue it onto the end of the stamen. Tape the flower to the stem with clear tape or green florist tape to hold it firm. ✢

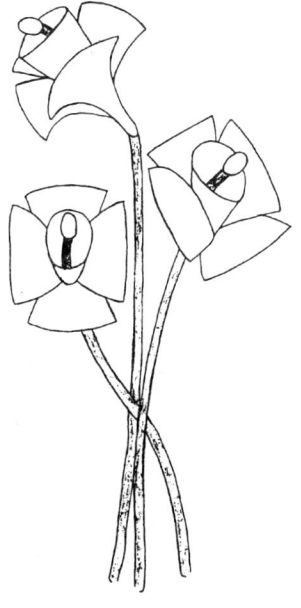

Lenten Cross

by Deborah Payden

Here is a good project to do at the beginning of the Lenten season.

1. Take two craft sticks and hold them together to form a cross.

2. Take a piece of yarn. Begin to wrap the yarn around the middle of the cross where the two sticks meet. Make sure to leave a length of yarn free to tie after you done wrapping the yarn around the middle.

3. Wrap the yarn diagonally one way, then diagonally the other way until the two sticks are secure.

4. Take the end of the piece of yarn and tie it to the free end you left at the beginning. Tie a knot in the yarn on the backside of the cross you have made.

5. Place a small nail through the yarn. This nail will serve as a reminder during Lent of the suffering and death of Jesus. It is a sad cross.

6. Put your cross in a place so you will see it all during Lent.

7. On Easter morning, take the nail out before you do anything else! Now you have a resurrection cross to remind you that God is so powerful that even death cannot separate us from God's love. Alleluia Christ is Risen!

(If you would like to make more Lenten crosses, you can do so using straws, popsicle sticks, or small branches from trees.) ✢

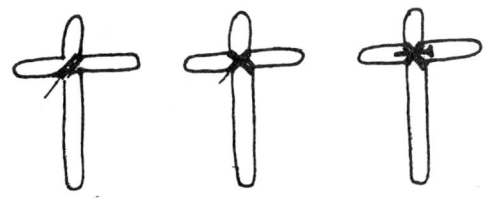

Palm Sunday Echo Pantomime

by Deborah Payden

SCRIPT	ACTIONS
Jesus set his face toward Jerusalem	*Start with head bowed then lift and turn head to the right.*
Jesus said to his disciples,	*Face front and shake finger as it talking to someone.*
Go into that village.	*Point with finger and arm straight ahead and walk in place.*
You will find a donkey.	*Hands shielding eyes as if looking and move head from left to right.*
Bring it to me.	*Beckon with arms toward self*
The disciples went and found the donkey.	*Shake head "yes"and pretend to pull a donkey with a rope.*
Jesus got on the donkey.	*Pretend to be climbing onto the donkey.*
He rode the donkey into Jerusalem.	*Pretend to ride a horse gently by bending up and down at knees.*
People threw their coats down for the donkey.	*Pretend to take off a coat or cape and throw to the ground*
Other people waved Palm branches.	*Wave arms high back and forth like waving branches*
The people shouted "Hosanna, Hosanna."	*Shout "Hosanna" after reader is done as arms continue to wave branches.*
"Blessed is he who comes in the name of the Lord."	*Bow low as if to a King.*
"Peace in heaven and Glory in the highest heaven."	*Sweep arms in front of body, crossing and up over head, lift head upward.*
Some Pharisees did not like the people shouting.	*Hands on hips, stamp one foot, shake head "no", and look angry*
They told Jesus to make the people stop.	*Palms of hands facing out and push straight out away from body.*
Jesus said: "If they stop, even the stones in the earth would shout out."	*Smile, then look down and point fingers to the ground. Then lift face front, and shout "Hosanna" after reader is finished.* ✟

Easter Egg Art Project

by Teresa Baggot

Materials needed: For each student, a large sheet of construction paper on which is drawn a large egg. Scissors, pencils, crayons, paintbrushes, watercolor paints, water for dipping, newspapers for work surfaces.

Introduce this crayon resist art project by discussing Easter symbols, such as the egg (symbolic of new life), the empty tomb (Christ has risen), the Easter lily (blossoming), butterfly (emerging from darkness of cocoon) and sunrise (bringing light to darkness). Write each upon chalkboard for reference.

Distribute art materials and ask students to cut out the egg and draw and color some or all of the Easter symbols on it, leaving some uncolored areas. After they are finished, they are to paint over the entire egg with the watercolor paints, either one color or several. ✞

Plant A Sign For Christ

by Virginia Fleishans

When parishioners arrive for services on Easter Sunday, their celebration will begin the minute they see colorful crosses and signs "planted" in the grass throughout the church grounds or campus.

Church school teachers will welcome this simple project because it allows the children to positively impact the adult celebration of worship. Brightly colored paper signs with messages such as "He Is Risen," "Christ the King," "Christ is Lord," "He Lives!" and "Easter Joy," can be cut into circles, squares, triangles, or egg shapes, then glued on popsicle sticks. Popsicle sticks can also be decorated and glued together as celebration crosses. The signs and crosses are then "planted" in grass or soft soil in the parking lot, courtyard, or front lawn of your church. The more signs and crosses you plant, the more effective the message!

The popsicle sticks won't hurt the lawn and can be easily removed the same day—possibly by the same children who planted them. The gardener may even thank you for helping to aerate the soil! ✞

Section Three Youth

Understanding Death

by Elaine M. Ward

"If a man die, shall he live again?" Job asked. Robert McAfee Brown gives six answers to that question:[1]

- The "realistic" factual response: "When you are dead, you are dead. We only live once, let us make the most of it."
- The "pie-in-the-sky-when-you-die" attitude: "Life on earth doesn't matter. I'm waiting for heaven."
- The "living on in the memories of others" evasion: immortality of influence.
- The "wheel of existence" theory: reincarnation, being born again in another form.
- The "immortality of the soul": the body is a nuisance to the soul which will continue to exist.
- The biblical approach affirms that God has created us for relationship. Sin, which is separation from God, and death, which is separation from life, are related in the Bible.

The Old Testament writers first saw death as total separation from God in the "pit," Sheol, where God was not present.

"I am reckoned among those who go down to the Pit; like those whom thou dost remember no more." (Ps. 88:4-5)

There is a later view, however, that expresses their trust that God can even reach into Sheol. Jonah said that even if he made his bed in hell, God would find him there, and the psalmist sang, "If I make my bed in Sheol, thou art there!"

The New Testament has no doubt. God's power is greater than the power of death. "I am making all things new," is the last biblical promise.

Paul wrote of a "spiritual body," a total personality, which would be made new: "What is sown is perishable, what is raised is imperishable...it is sown a physical body, it is raised a spiritual body" (1 Corinthians 15:42-44).

Several years ago, teaching a sixth grade confirmation class on the question of life after death, "Will I live again?" I used Brown's list but translated the ideas into narrative form. The story, "Anna's Answer" is that narrative:

"Something or someone was following Anna through the dark hallway to her room. Each night, as she ran up the dark stairway, she heard strange sounds. "There are no ghosts," Anna spoke aloud in the dark. When the door suddenly banged shut, however, Anna jumped into bed. Under her bedsheets she felt safer. Whatever was "out there" couldn't reach her under the sheets, but Anna no sooner thought this than she knew it was as silly as believing that there were ghosts in the dark.

Perhaps she should stop watching scary television shows, as her mother had said. "Tomorrow I will not visit Maria after school!" Anna promised herself.

Maria was one of Anna's friends, and very special, for she could tell bewitching stories that enchanted (and frightened) Anna.

The next afternoon, in the bright sunlight after school, however, Anna forgot her fear and her promise of the night before, and as usual stopped to visit Maria. Anna had a question she wanted answered.

"What will happen to me when I die?" Anna asked Maria. She had been thinking about it for some time, and it may have been the reason she was afraid in the dark.

Maria turned her head quickly to see if anyone was listening. Then, putting her finger to her lips for silence, she motioned Anna to follow her.

The two girls tiptoed down the path. When they entered the woods behind Maria's house, Maria stopped to listen. "Wait here," she whispered, disappearing into the trees.

Even though the sun was shining outside the woods, inside the woods it was dark. Anna shuddered, wondering why she had followed Maria.

"Come!" Maria commanded, as she took Anna's hand and led her toward the rocks.

"Where...are we...going?"

Maria pointed to a large hole in the rocks that Anna had not noticed before. It was a hollow cave. Maria pushed Anna into the cave before there was time to ask any more questions.

For a few moments neither girl spoke. "Have you ever heard of 'reincarnation'?" Maria asked in a whisper.

Anna shook her head "no."

"When you die, you will be reborn," said Maria. "If you are bad, you may be reborn as a dog. If you are very bad, as a chicken or a rat!"

Anna made a face, thinking of the chicken they had eaten last Sunday. What if that had been Aunt Minnie?

"What happens if you are good?"

"If you are good enough, as you work up the scale, you are finally purified and escape living at all."

"I don't believe..." escaped from Anna. "I mean...thank you for answering my question. Can we go now?"

"Do not tell anyone where you have been. This is my secret place," said Maria, as they left the cave and returned to the sunlight.

"Pure poppy-cock!" said Uncle Oscar, as he listened to his niece tell him what Maria had told her. Every Saturday afternoon Uncle Oscar and Anna went to the ice cream parlor together.

Uncle Oscar sputtered into his soda, "Everyone who is honest knows you only live once. You are born, live, and die, and that's all there is to it! The sooner people face the stark, stern reality of death, the better for all of us!"

Anna had never seen or heard her uncle so angry. "Why are you so upset, Uncle Oscar?"

"I am not upset! I don't like to talk about death. Eat your ice cream. We are going home!"

Anna was silent, as they drove home. "I wonder what is the matter with Uncle Oscar?" she asked herself.

Her grandmother asked the same question, when they reached home.

"I don't know. We were talking about death and he got upset and said we only live once, make the most of it and don't rock the boat," Anna replied.

Grandmother shook her head sadly. "Yes, your Uncle Oscar and I have had many talks, many arguments about his 'row, row, row your boat' attitude."

"What, Grandma?"

"You know the song, 'Row, row, row your boat, gently down the stream. Merrily, merrily, merrily, life is but a dream,'" said Grandma. "Uncle Oscar lives as if there were no tomorrow, but everyone knows one should live a good life, that all the suffering in this life will be rewarded with heaven."

"Uncle Oscar calls that 'pie-in-the-sky-when-you-die' nonsense," said Anna's father, as he walked into the room, having heard his mother talking with Anna. "He says it is like getting a lollipop for being a good boy at the dentist's."

"Do you agree?" Anna was becoming very confused with so many different answers. If only there were just one answer!

"No, I don't agree with either of them," Father explained. "We live a good life in order to influence others. We live on in the memories of others, because of our ideas, our personality, and our deeds. Why, Abraham Lincoln is as alive as he ever was, in the hearts of his people."

"What about Aunt Minnie?" Grandmother asked. "How many people will remember her in a hundred years, when we are dead and gone?"

Anna squirmed uncomfortably, remembering how she had imagined Aunt Minnie as their Sunday dinner.

That night Anna dreamed about what might happen to her when she died. When she awakened the next morning, she was upset. "Mr. Bishop may be able to help me," Anna said, sitting up in her bed, determined that today she would find the answer to her question. Mr. Bishop was Anna's teacher at school.

"I believe, Anna," he said, when asked, "that there is a part of me called my soul that continues to live after I am dead. My soul lives in my body, but when I no longer need my body, my soul is released for immortality. It is like outgrowing a suit or a dress."

That made sense! Anna felt a sense of relief. She was glad she had asked.

That afternoon she shared it with Mary. "It sounds good to me, Mary. What do you think?" Anna trusted Mary. Mary had come once a week to help her mother for as long as Anna could remember. All her life Anna had known that Mary knew what was best for her. "Mary, what do you think?" Anna repeated. "What do you think will happen to me when I die?"

"I think our bodies are important, Anna, and so is our life right now, but when we die, Anna, our bodies will be changed."

"How, Mary? How will they change?"

"Have you ever watched a farmer sow grain?"

"No," Anna replied.

"Have you ever planted a seed?"

"Oh, yes!" Anna replied.

"The seed in the ground dies. When the wheat, or flower, or vegetable grows, the seed is changed. The seed is different from the flower. The dead body is like that. Paul said in the Bible that it is sown a 'physical' body and raised a 'spiritual' body. That is what I believe."

"When I am dead, will you know me, Mary?" Anna said, throwing her arms around Mary's neck.

"Yes, child, I will know you, for both of us will be with God."

"I thought that we were with God now?"

"Yes, child, we are with God now. That is why nothing can keep us apart from God when we die. Amen!"

"Amen!" added Anna, her mind swimming with answers and glad for Mary and for her love and presence. But most of all for the knowledge of God's love and presence here and now...and yet to come!

CONVERSATION TOPICS:

1. Tell or read and discuss Anna's story.

2. Discuss the six varieties of beliefs about what happens after death. Knowing our beliefs can change, what are your current beliefs about what happens after death? What are your doubts?

3. Using concordances, look up biblical references concerning death and discuss their meanings.

4. At the entrance to the tunnel of "death" place a large paper cross. Ask participants to write their concerns, sins, worries, things they want to "die" within them or in the world on small pieces of paper to pin or tape to the cross before they enter the "dark" tunnel. Walk or crawl through the tunnel. As they emerge, present them "wings" of transformation, new life.

5. Spend a few moments in guided faith meditation prayer. Place feet flat on the floor, put hands in laps, close eyes, and take three deep breaths. After a few moments of silence, imagine: You are in a garden. It is quiet. You observe the green grass, the pink flowers blooming, the touch of their soft petals and their fragrance. As you enjoy the beauty of the garden, Christ enters and sits beside you. As you talk together, you ask him to help you make a decision about something in your life right now. Perhaps you have hurt someone and wish to ask for forgiveness, or you need something and want to tell him about that. Maybe you just want to talk and thank him or sit in silence, enjoying his presence. Take time to let thoughts and images flow in and out of your consciousness. *(Pause for a long period of silence)* Suddenly Christ kneels to pray and you join him. When you are finished praying together, you ask him a question, any question you want to ask, and he smiles and replies. *(Pause)* When Jesus leaves, breathe quietly in the stillness. Feel the strength within you. Think about what you will do because of what has happened. *(Pause)* Then slowly return to the room and open your eyes.

6. Close with reading Romans 8:37-39 as an affirmation of faith, sing "Amazing Grace" and pray 1 Corinthians 15:55,57.

---

[1]Robert McAfee Brown, The Bible Speaks to You, (Philadephia: Westminster Press, MCMLV).

Lent: Not Death But Renewed Life

by Terry Deffenbaugh

In Middle English Lent means spring time. It is a time of renewal. Not only in the world around us but also in our own lives. It is a perfect time for a youth group to focus on both group and individual renewal. Each week is set up to focus on a different part of the renewal process.

These ideas are not meant to be the whole session but rather to be part of a teen session. If at all possible it would be nice to actually have a flower pot and live plant. Make it a plain clay pot as you will decorate it later in Lent. You might use seeds, a young plant, crocus or paperwhite bulbs. These are the quickest to grow and bloom. You might also talk to a gardener and see what he/she suggests for your area.

Week 1: PREPARING THE SOIL

If anything is going to grow well the soil that it grows in has to be ready to aid in that growth. All of the rocks that make the soil resistant to growth has to be gotten rid of. If we are going to have renewal in our lives then we need to first prepare ourselves for that renewal. We need to take a serious look at our lives and see what we need to get rid of which is keeping us from that new growth.

What this first week of Lent invites us to do is to have an attitude adjustment. We need to get rid of the rocks in our lives that keep us from growing.

Before the youth come in have a pile of stones in a flowerpot. They should be different sizes and colors. Have no stone bigger than two inches in diameter. Also make sure that the stones are clean.

When the teens arrive, have them pick up a stone of their choosing, and hold it in their hand. They may not put it down or in their pockets. After everyone is there, remind them that they may not put down the rock for any reason. Then just go on with your normal session as it usually is done. If anyone asks about the rock simply tell them that it will all make sense later.

At the end of the session explain to the teens that Lent is a time of growth and renewal. In order to have a field open for growth it must first of all be cleared of rocks. Explain that probably in each of our lives there are many rocks that keep us from being as good as we can! Read John 8:1-10. Ask the teens to go somewhere in the room alone and reflect on what the stone might represent in their life which is keeping their relationships with God and others from growing stronger. They are to decide in this time of Lent what one attitude adjustment that they are going to work on. Maybe they have to work on patience or not putting things off, etc. When they come back, invite them to share with the group what the stone represents and how they are going to work on it during Lent. Be sure not to pressure anyone to share if they prefer to keep it to themself. Tell the teens that you would like them to keep the stone with them during Lent, if possible in their purse or pocket. Or at least keep it somewhere in their room that will remind them what they have decided to work on.

End by reading John 8:11. Tell them that the stone will be used later in Lent.

Week 2: GOOD SEED

The second week of Lent is for the planting of the good seeds. It is in faith that we believe that by putting a good seed in the ground that it will grow and become fruitful. You might also ask how they are doing with what the stone represents for them.

In the second week the young people should be challenged to look at the ways in which God has blessed them and take inventory. This is best done at the beginning of the session because it is hard to predict how long it will take the teens to do the second part.

Give each youth a piece of paper. Have the teens put their name on the paper and ask them to take a little time to write on the paper those God-given qualities of which they are proud. Tell them to be honest and serious about the goodness that they see in their life. Also warn them that this will be read by some of the other people in the group. Give them about three minutes to do this.

The next part is where you will have to know your group and how serious they can be. Tell them that often we do not see our own goodness or in false humility not recognize what God has given us. Collect all of the papers, mix them up and pass them back out. No one is to get their own paper. After you have done this ask the teens to go and sit by themselves and to add at least one other quality that they see in the person whose paper they have. Remind them to take this seriously for what they are doing is affirming the goodness that God has created in that person. They are not to sign it. Do this several times. Then give everyone their own paper back and ask them to look at what has been added. Invite anyone who wishes to share how they feel seeing other qualities listed on their paper which were added by someone else.

Explain to the youth that God has created in each of us good seeds to make the world a better place. That we need to recognize the good and have faith that it will grow. At this time plant some type of bulb, seeds or plant. After the planting read Matthew 13:31-32. As you water the seed you might remind the teens of the life-giving water that is used at baptisms.

Their lists are the seeds in their lives. Have them take their paper home with them and look them over during the week. Ask them to make sure to bring them back next week because they will be needed for the next session.

Week 3: EXPANDING LIFE

If a seed stays nothing more than a seed it is a waste. Its potential has been destroyed. In the same way if we do not use our God-given talents beyond ourself it is a waste. God has given us gifts not to be horded but rather to be used by the whole church. It is this expanding of the potential that we have been given that makes us a mission church. We send out roots to help make a firm grounding of our faith and shoots to expand the message of Jesus Christ.

If at all possible remind the teens to bring their inventory list from the last session. You might like to use this at the beginning of the session so you will have enough time to do the brain storming that is used in this session. As the teens come in check to make sure they have their inventory from the last session. If they did not bring them, have them quickly write down their inventory list so that they can use it in this session.

Read Luke 19:6. Remind the teens that gifts are not given just to us, but rather to use to help others. Ask each teen to take out their inventory of their blessings. Ask them to circle one of them that they would like to look at in a more intense way. After they have done this ask them to come up with some concrete ways in which that talent can be shared to make their world, school, parish, youth group and family better. Give them about five minutes to come up with some ideas. If they finish early, have them come up with ideas for another one of their strengths. After the time is up, have all of the teens come back into a larger circle. Ask if anyone had any trouble coming up with some concrete ideas. If anyone did have problems, invite them to share with the group what the quality was and see if the group can come up with any ideas.

When this is finished tell the teens that they now have to share with the group one way they will work on sharing that quality for the rest of Lent. Ask them to note it on their list so that they can put it next to the rock to now remember they have both a negative and positive that they are working on this Lent.

At the end of this session make sure that the plant that you have been using has the right amount of water and is in either the sun or under a grow light. Remind the teens that as the water will give life to the plants so too will the light. Just as Jesus is our light and gives us the courage to spread our gifts so too will the plant spread its roots and sprout.

Week 4: THE WEAK BECOME STRONG

In all of nature to heal is to make stronger. When we heal a broken bone it becomes stronger. In the same way a plant will heal a wound by growing more in that area, even to the point that two limbs will grow together making one.

This week is for asking forgiveness and being forgiven. Every time we have people gather together we can have hurt feelings. It can happen accidentally with thoughtlessness or it can be on purpose out of anger. If a youth group and the individuals in a youth group are to grow stronger, it is important that all of this pain is healed.

This might be done at the end of a session unless there is a need for a lot of reconciliation. Have the teens come together in one large circle. Tell the teens that you do not want anyone to point to anyone else but to be honest. Ask anyone who feels they have had their feelings hurt by anyone in the group on purpose or accidentally to raise their hand. Then ask if anyone feels that someone else has misjudged them or been mean to them to raise their hand. Next ask that if anyone feels that they have probably hurt someone else's feelings, either on purpose or accidentally, to raise their hand. And finally ask for anyone who feels that they have misjudged or been mean to someone in the group to raise their hand. Most often everyone has raised their hand for at least one of the four categories. Tell the teens that we are going to be given a chance to take care of all of that pain.

The youth are to take a moment to think of all of the things which they have done to hurt someone else in this group, talking behind someone else's back, teasing to the point of hurting or being mean. They may not have meant to hurt someone else, but that is incidental. If they did hurt someone else, challenge them to have the courage to admit it to themselves.

Next they will turn their chairs facing out. When the music comes on tell them that they will have a chance to get up, go to someone else and tap them on the shoulder, inviting them into the center of circle to take care of business. They are to apologize for what they have done. This is to be done only loud enough for the person to hear, not loud enough for everyone to hear. They will not take turns, rather when the music comes on, if they have some apologizing to do, they are to get up. If they have to apologize to more than one person they need to move faster. If they get up to see someone and that person is with someone already, they are to wait their turn. No crowds, only one on one. If they need to apologize to everyone in the group, they are not to come to the center of the group and say, "I'm Sorry"; there will be a time to talk to the whole group, but not yet. Use whatever reconciliation music you feel is best for your group. Try "From a Distance" by Bette Midler. While they are doing this, walk around the center of the group to make sure no one is mocking the seriousness of this reconciliation service.

When this is finished have them turn their chairs facing in. Now is the time for group apologies. Maybe someone has misjudged the whole group, or had an attitude which affected everyone. It can be done by simply going around the group and having anyone speak who wants to, passing if they have nothing to say. Or you can simply ask if anyone would like to speak to the whole group to stand and do so.

When everyone is finished, read Luke 15:11-32. Then bring the teens around the plant and put in a stake and tie the young plant to it so that it will have more support. Explain that the group supports each other by forgiving each other.

Week 5: BUDDING

At this time in a plant's life we see the promise of the beauty that is to come. It is a time of anticipation and also a time of seeing the promise of the seed becoming a reality.

Once again this might be best used at the end of a regular session. A similar technique from last week will be used but in a different way. Have the teens form one large circle as they did last week but with the chairs facing in. Tell them that we all grow because of each other and as last week it was important to say "I'm sorry." It is also important to thank those people who have been friends, who have challenged us and been there for us in bad times.

Ask them to take a moment to look around and think of all the people in this circle who have helped them in any way. Tonight they will be given a chance to thank those people. Tell them that when the music comes on, if there is anyone to whom they feel they owe a thank you, get up and take care of business. If they need to thank more than one person, they are to move quicker. But they are not to go into the center of the group and yell, "Thank you everyone." There will be a chance to thank the whole group, but not yet. Tell them that this time everyone will be facing in. If they get up to thank someone who is already being talked to, wait their turn, no crowds. What is said is only to be said loud enough for the person to hear. It is best to be specific as to why they are thanking the person. Maybe that person was there when they were having problems at home or with another friend. When the music stops they are to go back to their chair. As you did last week, be walking around in the center of the group to make sure that no one is mocking this time of affirmation. Use what ever affirmation music works best with your group. Try "Wind Beneath My Wings" by Bette Midler.

After the music has ended and everyone is sitting down, tell the teens that maybe some need to thank the whole group for helping them grow and develop into the Christian that they have become. Go around the group and let anyone say anything that they feel moved to say. If some have nothing to say, then they should simply say pass.

When this is finished, gather the teens around the plant and give the plant a little bit of plant food. Remind the teens that affirmation is always something to grow on. End by reading Matthew 5:3-12.

Week 6: ANTICIPATION

This week begins with Palm Sunday. It is a time of watching and waiting. It is when we are to make the final preparation for the budding forth of new life. In many parishes everything slows down in this week as a total parish preparation. You have to know what your parish traditions are. It is also a good time to go over each week of Lent and have the teens reflect on what they have learned and how they have grown. I suggest that at least you invite the teens to bring back the stones and use them to decorate the planter which has been the focus of these six weeks. Remind them that in the Gospel they put the stones down. It might be good to read again that passage from the first week, John 8:1-11. This week is meant to be rather low key other than the activities of Holy Thursday, Good Friday and Holy Saturday. If you would like other ideas on how to make Holy Week even more involved for your teens, I might recommend the book Come, Watch With Me, published by Educational Ministries, Inc. In this book I take all of the days from Palm Sunday until Pentecost and make each of them mini-retreats. You might like to end this session by reading Luke 21:34-38.

(Continued on page 94)

A Lenten Journey

by Deborah Payden

During the Sundays of Lent, the children and youth in our congregation lead us through a Lenten Journey. As a part of the Sunday liturgy we are reminded by word and symbol each week of the events surrounding the passion and death of Jesus. These events of Holy Week are also to serve as reminders of how we are presently involved in those events.

A youth reads the scripture each Sunday from one of the Gospels pertaining to a Holy Week event. Following the reading of scripture there is a brief interpretation read that lifts up the significance of that event in our lives today. Following this reading, a symbol is shown to the congregation as a reminder of that particular event. This symbol is given to a small child who places it at the base of a cross, designated as our "Lenten Cross." Each week symbols are added to the cross.

On Easter Sunday, the symbols have been removed and the Lenten Journey that appeared in the bulletin Liturgy is now replaced by an Easter Journey. The scripture read this day is from one of the Epistles and shares the significance of the resurrection in our lives. The symbol placed on the cross is a butterfly.

Here is a selected list of scriptures and symbols we have use for our Lenten Journey.

First Sunday—taken from John 13 (towel)
Second Sunday—Matthew 26:69-75 (rooster)
Third Sunday—excerpts from Mark 14 (cup and loaf)
Fourth Sunday—Matthew 26:14-16 (money bag)
Fifth Sunday—Matthew 29:19 (palm branch)
Palm Sunday—Matthew 26:27-31(crown of thorns)
Easter—excerpts from I Peter 1 (butterfly)

1st Sunday in Lent

Today we begin our Lenten journey. It is a journey that will remind us of the events of Holy Week. Each Sunday we will have a reading based on a Bible scripture, followed by a symbol placed by a Lenten cross.

Our scripture today is taken from the Gospel of John, chapter 13. *Jesus rose from the table, took off his outer garment and tied a towel around his waist. Then he poured water into a basin and began to wash the disciples' feet, and dry them with the towel around his waist. After he had washed their feet, he returned to his place at the table. "Do you understand what I have just done to you?" he asked. "You call me Teacher and Lord, and it is right that you do so, because that is what I am. I, your Lord have just set an example for you, so that you will do just what I have done for you.* In this scripture, Jesus reminds us that we are to be servants to one another. No one is more important than anyone else. To be a follower of Jesus is to be a servant to others. We are called to help and take care of others. When we do this, we follow the example of Jesus. To remind us that we are servants for Christ, we place a towel by our Lenten cross.

2nd Sunday in Lent

Our scripture today is from Matthew 26:69-75. *Peter was sitting outside the courtyard when one of the High Priest's servant girls came to him and said, "You too, were with Jesus of Galilee." But Peter denied it saying, "I don't know what you are talking about!" Another servant girl saw Peter and said to the men there, "He was with Jesus of Nazareth." Again Peter denied it saying, "I swear that I don't know that man!" After awhile the men standing there came to Peter and said, "Of course you are one of them!" Then Peter said, "I swear that I am telling the truth! May God punish me if I am not. I do not know the man!" Just then a rooster crowed, and Peter remembered what Jesus had told him; "Before the cock crows you will say three times that you do not know me." Peter went out and cried bitterly.*

It is sometimes difficult to be a follower of Jesus. It is hard to live our lives caring for other people the way Jesus wants us to. We say we are disciples, followers of Jesus. But we do not always act or talk like we are disciples of Jesus. When we show others that we are followers of Jesus, we are like Peter. We deny Christ by our words and our actions. Today we place a toy rooster by our Lenten cross to remind us that sometimes we are like Peter and we pretend not to know Jesus.

3rd Sunday in Lent

Our scripture today is from Mark, chapter 14. *On the first day of the Festival of Unleavened Bread, the day the lambs were killed for Passover, Jesus' disciples asked him, "Where do you want us to go and get the Passover meal ready for you?" Then Jesus sent two of them into the city with instructions. The disciples left, went to the city and found everything just as Jesus had told them, and they prepared the Passover meal. While they were eating, Jesus took a piece of bread, gave thanks, broke it and gave it to his disciples. "Take it," he said, "this is my body." Then he took a cup, gave thanks to God, and handed it to them, and they drank from it. Jesus said, "This is my blood which is poured out for many, my blood which seals God's covenant."*

When we celebrate the Lord's Supper in church, we remember the Passover meal that Jesus had with his disciples. The Passover meal is a very special Jewish holiday. It celebrates the liberation of the Hebrew slaves, from the oppression of the Egyptians so very long ago. Jesus has freed us too. Communion reminds us of how Jesus gave his life for us so that we may be free to live our lives as God intends for us to live them. Today we place a cup and bread by our Lenten cross to remind us that when we celebrate the Lord's Supper, we are like the disciples that sat with Jesus at the passover meal so very long ago.

4th Sunday in Lent

Our scripture today is from Matthew 26:14-16. *Then one of the twelve disciples—the one named Judas—went to the chief priests and asked, "What will you give me if I betray Jesus to you?" They counted out thirty silver coins and gave them to him. From then on Judas was looking for a good chance to hand Jesus over to them.*

In the gospel of Mark we find that Judas finally betrayed Jesus with a kiss in the garden of Gethsemane.

It is not easy to be a follower of Jesus. We do not always understand what it means to be a disciple, or we do not like what Jesus wants us to do. Being a disciple of Jesus today still means that we are loyal and steadfast in our obedience to Christ. But there are times when being a follower of Jesus leads us to have to make difficult choices in life. Sometimes we chose an easier way to live our lives than to follow the way of the Christ. When we do this we are like Judas and we betray our faith, and our Christ. To remind us that we are sometimes like Judas, we place a money bag by our Lenten cross.

5th Sunday in Lent

Our scripture today is from Matthew 29:19. *As Jesus and his disciples approached Jerusalem, he sent two of the disciples on ahead with these instructions: "Go to the village there ahead of you and at once you will find a donkey with a colt tied up next to her. Untie them and bring them to me. And if anyone says anything say, "The Master has need of them, and them he will let them go at once." So the disciples went and did what Jesus had told them to do; they brought the donkey and the colt, threw their cloaks over them and Jesus got on. A large crowd of people spread their cloaks on the road while others cut branches from the trees and spread them on the road. The crowds walking in front of Jesus and those walking behind them on the road. The crowds walking in front of Jesus and those walking behind began to shout, "Praise to David's Son! God bless him who comes in the name of the Lord! Praise be to God!*

When Jesus entered Jerusalem he must have been filled with both joy and sadness. He knew what lie ahead of him there. But as he entered the city he was met with loud cheering and branches waving as he rode on the back of a donkey. He came into the city not as a proud war hero on a horse, but as a humble servant riding on a lowly donkey. Yet the people praised him as the one coming in the name of God. This is the one God has chosen to be the savior of God's people. The way of Jesus is the way of God. Sometimes we forget what Jesus is like. We need to be like the crowds in Jerusalem and shout praises to Jesus and greet him as our Savior. We place a palm branch by our Lenten cross to remind us that Jesus is the one that comes in the name of God into our lives today!

Palm Sunday

Our scripture for today is from Matthew 27:27-31. *Then Pilot's soldiers took Jesus into the governor's palace and the whole company gathered around him. They stripped off his clothes and put a scarlet robe on him. Then they made a crown of thorny branches and placed it on his head, and put a stick in his right hand; then they knelt before him and made fun of him. "Long live the King of the Jews!" they said. They spat on him, and took the stick and hit him on the head. When they had finished making fun of him, they took the robe off and put his own clothes back on him. Then they led him out to crucify him.*

Today is a happy and joyous day in the church. But it is also the beginning of Holy Week, the week in which we remember the betrayal, trial, mocking and death of Jesus. It is easy for us to forget the sad and dark parts of the story of Jesus. We do not like to remember Jesus being killed. We

(Continued on page 92)

Lenten Steps

by Miriam Perry

Youth are a "hands on" group. Lent is not a time of experiencing but a time of reflection for adults. The key to communication is to talk the language. The adult reflection needs to be translated into a tangible experience.

One method of providing this experience is to walk through Jesus' steps to the Cross with the students. This is not a drama to be presented, although it could be altered to accomplish that goal. Each major event is lived out, and discussed as they experience it. If the events are done as a strictly youth event, there will be more effort put into it by the youth, and discussion is easier.

The events I will outline are: Thursday night Passover Meal with washing of the feet by the leader and enactment of the betrayal of Judas and the arrest. Friday, the carrying of the cross to Calvary, the seven last words of Christ with character sketches of main figures.

This may be done during Holy Week, but its impact is almost greater if used as a preparation for Lent. It is suggested that the events be spread over an extended period, like a Friday night lock-in. If the event is to be spread over a two-three day period, you could add a fast to indicate death, broken by Easter Sunrise service with Resurrection theme.

As the youth gather, ask them to sit in a circle with their backs to one another, facing outward away from the tables which can be set for the Passover Meal.

THURSDAY EVENTS

WASHING OF THE FEET

1) After all the youth are seated, the leader comes in, without introduction begins to remove the shoes of a member and wash each foot.

2) Then the leader stands up and says to that youth, "As I have done this to you, do likewise to your neighbor."

3) Each youth in turn washes the feet of the neighbor to the right. (*If the group is large, there can be smaller circles, or the leader can pick various ones around the circle to then wash those and start another youth washing cycle.*)

DISCUSS:
- What was your first thought as someone undid your shoe and wanted to wash your feet? (Check what Peter's response was to this event?)
- How did the one who was doing the washing feel about touching someone else's feet?
- What does this teach us about servanthood? What did Jesus teach by this event?

PASSOVER MEAL
(served as a fellowship meal with discussion built into ceremony)

1) After all the feet have been washed and the discussion questions answered, along with other questions that may have been raised, turn the chairs around to face the tables.

2) Adults can serve the components of the Passover Meal. (See #1 of Optional Additions.) a) The green herb, b) The breaking of unleavened bread, c) The haroset and moror, d) The wine poured out.

3) The meal ends with prayer from John 17 and then singing as they group moves outside.

DISCUSS:
- Are you worried about what happens next? Did Jesus show concern?
- If the group is new to the Passover event, ask for questions about it.

PLAY OF THE BETRAYAL AND ARREST
(Works best if at night)

The group goes outside singing, with the leader in the front of the group with a flashlight. An adult portraying Judas, and two others as guards, come out from the other side of the building to confront the group. (*Keep the youth group unaware they were to come.*) The words and actions of the gospel story are found in Luke 22:47-53. Assign roles of Peter and John. a) Greeting with kiss by Judas, b) Peter cutting off guard's ear, leader healing it, c) Leader says Jesus' speech about leading a rebellion, and being led away, d) Peter and John follow, but the rest of the group scatters.

DISCUSS: (*Bring the group back inside to discuss.*)
- What was your emotion when the men came to get your leader?
- What was your thought about the betrayal, especially with a kiss?
- Did you feel like scattering sooner, or did you want to follow also?
- Have you had a leader who was falsely accused? When? Did you stand up for that person? Would you stand up for a student leader quicker than an adult leader?

FRIDAY EVENTS

CRUCIFIXION OF JESUS

1) Carrying the cross: Continue having the leader of the youth group portray Jesus. (*Use a cross with rough 2x4 wood pieces if possible. If there is a hill near the church, use this place to hold the Friday Events*)

DISCUSS: While the leader carries the cross up the hill, have student leaders discuss in small groups what the emotions of the disciples might be as they watch Jesus carrying the cross. (Did they want to help him? Were they afraid they would be asked to carry it? Were they proud to be a follower of this man?)

2) Nailing Jesus to the Cross: Tie the leader to the cross upright, leaning against a tree or rock. Make sure he is not hurt. Assign roles to the youth to portray various disciples, especially Mary, the Mother of Jesus, Mary Magdalene, Peter, and John. Have the youth group stand around as the crowd, with two as the other crucified men and also Roman guards. (*If they have roles, they will be less inclined to be distracted. The fewer props the more they have to concentrate on the action.*)

3) At the foot of the Cross with Jesus' Seven Last Words from Luke 23:32-49, John 19:25-30:

- As the leader is propped up on the cross, he says: "Father, forgive them, for they do not know what they are doing."
- The guards throw dice for who gets his robe.
- Mary Magdalene cries out: "Don't you care? You just stand there and gawk. What has he done to you? Has he ever brought you anything but good?" (See #2 of Optional Additions.)
- Two men crucified with the leader, (just standing there to emphasize the wrong) are having the dialogue from Luke 23:39-42. The leader responds in Jesus' words: "I tell you the truth, today you will be with me in paradise."
- Mary, Mother of Jesus, Mary, the wife of Clopas, and Mary Magdalene are near the foot of the cross with John. The leader says Jesus' words: "Dear woman, here is your son." (See #3 of Optional Additions.) And to John he said, "Here is your mother." (See #4 of Optional Additions.) John leads Mary away, and the other women follow.
- After some time the leader repeats Jesus words: "My God, my God, why have you forsaken me?" (See #5 of Optional Additions.)
- Later the leader says Jesus' words: "I am thirsty." A guard takes a sponge on a stick to give him a drink of vinegar.
- After receiving the drink the leader says the words: "It is finished."
- Then an earthquake occurred, and the leader quotes Jesus who called out with a loud voice, "Father, into your hands I commit my spirit." When he had said this, he breathed his last.

At this point, depending on the mood of the group, allow some silent time, with the leader still on the cross. Then remove the leader from the cross and allow him or her to rest, gathering the group around.

DISCUSS:
- What did the disciples do during this time, except for John? How do you think they felt about this in activity? How do you think they felt about John?
- The guard having seen Jesus die stated: "Surely this was a righteous man." Do you think he came to believe in Jesus as his Savior?
- Jesus cried out, "My God, my God, why have you forsaken me?" Do you think God really forsook his Son? What really was happening here that is the basis of our salvation?

Optional Additions:

1. The Passover meal can be just the elements of the Seder as outlined here, or it may be an entire Seder Meal as included in the appendix.

2. Mary Magdalene can give a monologue as provided

if the students want in-depth feelings.

    I, Mary, watched the guards throw the dice on the ground. Jesus' robe lay in a pile beside the one. As soon as the game was ended, the winner grabbed the robe and flung it over his shoulders. It was disgusting to me. I turned aside to stand near the cross with His mother and aunt. How could they be so insensitive? I looked at the crowd milling about the area. "Don't you care? You just stand there and gawk. What has he done to you? Has he ever brought you anything but good?" All at once my heart became quiet. He's done only good to me. I, the greatest of sinners, have received forgiveness and kindness and mercy which I do not deserve. I deserve to die for my adulterous sins, not Him. He loves everyone. This is His only fault. My mind drifted back to the first time I had seen Jesus. A shiver ran up my spine at the thought of what I carried in my body in those days. Some said that I had seven devils. I only knew the pain that tormented me day and night. I was ugly and hateful because of it. Yet from the very first moment I looked into Jesus' eyes, I knew He loved me. I squirmed as He touched me. His touch was warm, no, hot, to my cold body. I could feel the coldness drain out of me. The warmth that I felt near His hand soon crept over my whole body, and I fell quietly at His feet. I was in a daze. He picked me up and said, "Be healed." What a day that was! What a day this is! I can hardly believe what has happened to Jesus. Yet He loved me and took my pain. I wish I could do the same for Him. I love you, Jesus. I love you.

3. Mary Mother of Jesus can give a monologue as provided.

    I, Mary, Mother of Jesus, wife of Joseph, have kept many things in my heart for many years. I love you. I don't know why these men did this to you. I am here for you. Yes, my son, I hear you. You want me to go home with John. Whatever you say. You know what is best. From the day that you were a small babe in my arms until the day Joseph died, I cared for you. My sweet Baby Jesus. How my heart aches to hold you again. But you grew up and became the head of our house, and you took care of my needs. When you began your ministry to the people, I hardly saw you. I believe you are the Messiah. How can this be? Why? Why, God? The words of the angel Gabriel came to mind. He had said: "He will be great and will be called the Son of the Most High. The Lord God will give him the throne of his father David." (Luke 1:32) Lord God, how can this be true with my Jesus hanging here before me on this cross? Then the angel's last words came to mind. "Nothing is impossible with God." I don't know how He can reign forever, but I believe in you, God, and I believe that He is your Son. If anything is possible out of this mess, it will be true for your Son. Even though there is a sword in my heart, O God, I believe what You said.

4. John can give a monologue as provided.

    Yes, Lord. I hear your request. I will take your mother home with me. I will care for her like she was my own mother. I love you, Lord. I will love her for your sake. I look into those eyes of love and I cannot help Him. He is hanging there on this cross and I did nothing to stop this from happening. I'm not a man. I am not worthy to be trusted to take care of this most precious woman. Yet I know He loves me. I sat by His side at the Passover and I knew He loved me. He who was with God from the beginning of time loved me, and now He hangs dying on the cross. I cannot help Him. At least I can do this thing for Him, so He won't worry about His mother. After Peter and I went with Him to the Mount, where He was transfigured into dazzling white apparel, I knew something was up. Moses and Elijah met Him there and they spoke of the time of suffering. I didn't know what they meant, but this must be it. If He can talk to Moses, why can't God just take Him down from this cross? Why can't He skip this part, and just get the radiant white robe of the after-life? Why does He have to die here?

5. Peter can give a monologue as provided.

    I, Peter, do not deserve to be here at your cross, Jesus. I denied you. I told the guards and the maid that I did not even know the man. I could not even say your name. I said that I did not know you, my Lord and my Master. I had said that they did not know what they were saying. I swore using an oath, as if I knew what I was saying. I was wrong. I have sinned against you, my Christ, my Messiah. I have sinned, but there you hang. I cannot bear to look. It is my fault. If I had spoken up for you, this would not have happened. I am awful. I deserve to die, not you. God has forsaken you? How could God do that to His Only Son? No! No! God, don't forsake Him. What does He have left? Who does He have on His side? Not me. How I wish it were all different. If only I could take back my words, and do the right thing. God, don't forsake Him. How will He bear all that sin by Himself? My sin is so great. I cannot bear it. Don't forsake Him, God. He has to bear all our sin. Where is forgiveness? There must be another way. God help Him. God help me.

APPENDIX

CHRISTIAN FEAST OF THE PASSOVER SEDER*

    L=Leader; C=Congregation; P=Parent; Y=Youth

Meaning Of The Seder Meal
L: The Passover meal is an ancient celebration of the

Jew's release from Egyptian bondage. The meal is called "Seder," which means "order," as in "the order of worship." The night before he was crucified, Jesus shared the Passover Seder with his disciples.

The Seder is a living experience of freedom. It is a renewal of life and values. May the words and events of this evening, taken from the language of flesh and blood, from physical and material reality, be a gateway for you to experience movement from death and bondage to life and freedom.

By eating together and sharing conversation, we remember God's continuing, mighty gift of freedom and life. So this evening, celebrate and enjoy! And remember, that in sharing these common experiences, we are worshiping God.

Now in the presence of one another, before us the elements of festive rejoicing, we gather for our sacred celebration. With believers, young and old, linking the past with the future, we listen again to God's call to service. Living our story that is told for all peoples, whose conclusion is yet to unfold, we gather to observe the Passover, as it is written:

C: YOU SHALL KEEP THE FEAST OF THE UNLEAVENED BREAD, FOR ON THIS VERY DAY I BROUGHT YOUR ANCESTORS OUT OF EGYPT. YOU SHALL OBSERVE THIS DAY THROUGHOUT THE GENERATIONS AS A PRACTICE FOR ALL TIMES.

L: We gather to celebrate our faith in the what is yet-to- be.

C: REMEMBER THE DAY ON WHICH YOU WENT FORTH FROM EGYPT, FROM THE HOUSE OF BONDAGE, AND HOW THE LORD FREED YOU WITH A MIGHTY HAND.

Light the Festive Candles of Hope
L: Blessed are you, the light of the world. As these candles light our festival of the Passover and the Last Supper, may Jesus light our lives as well. May the candles inspire us to use our powers to heal and not to harm, to help and not to hinder, to bless and not to curse, to serve you, O God of freedom.

(Turn all room lights off.)

The Sabbath Prayer
P: Blessed are you, O Lord God, King of the Universe, who has kept us alive, sustained us, and enabled us to reach this holy season. You have chosen us; you have given us this holy festival with loving kindness and blessed us with your favor.

C: AMEN

The First Cup Of Wine

(poured but do not drink yet)
L: Our story tells us that in diverse ways, with different words, God gave promises of freedom to those who have gone before us. (Exodus 6:6-8) With cups of wine we recall each one of them, as now, the first:

C: AS IT IS WRITTEN: "I AM THE LORD, AND I WILL FREE YOU FROM THE BURDENS OF THE EGYPTIANS."

L: We take up this cup and proclaim the holiness of the deliverance that comes from God. Many long years ago our ancestors obeyed the call to freedom. Tonight the same call is made to us. We are to arise and be free, and champion the cause of freedom and justice on behalf of all people. Let us raise our cups in gratitude to God that this call can still be heard in the land. Let us pray that the time will not be distant when all the world will be set free from cruelty, tyranny, war and oppression.

C: WE PRAISE YOU, GOD OF THE UNIVERSE, WHO CREATES THE FRUIT OF THE VINE. WE PRAISE YOU, OUR GOD, WHO HAS KEPT US IN LIFE, SUSTAINED US, AND BROUGHT US TO THIS FESTIVE SEASON.

(All drink the first cup of wine.)

Eating the Green Herb
L: Let us take a piece of celery, dip it in salt water, and bless the greens as the symbol of Spring.

C: PRAISED ARE YOU, O GOD, GOD OF THE UNIVERSE, WHO CREATES THE FRUIT OF THE EARTH.

L: The green vegetable symbolizes new life. The salt water symbolizes the tears and sweat of suffering during captivity in Egypt. Dipping the greens in salt water is a symbol for new life coming from the sweat and suffering of the past.

C: PRAISE BE TO YOU, O LORD OUR GOD, RULER OF THE UNIVERSE, CREATOR OF THE FRUIT OF THE EARTH.

(All eat the celery.)

Breaking of the Bread (Matzah)
L: Now I break the bread. Among the people everywhere, sharing of bread forms a bond of community. For the sake of our salvation, we join now with one another and with all who are in need because our salvation is bound up with the deliverance from bondage of people everywhere.

C: THIS IS THE BREAD OF AFFLICTION, THE POOR BREAD, WHICH OUR ANCESTORS ATE IN THE LAND OF EGYPT. LET ALL WHO ARE HUNGRY COME AND EAT. LET ALL WHO ARE IN WANT SHARE OUR HOPE. AS WE CELEBRATE HERE, WE JOIN WITH PEO-

PLE EVERYWHERE. MAY ALL BE FREE.

(All eat a piece of Matzah.)

L: This meal calls us to put an end to all slavery, both within and around us.

The Second Cup of Wine
(poured but do not drink yet)
L: With the second cup of wine we recall the second promise of liberation:

C: AS IT IS WRITTEN: "I WILL DELIVER YOU FROM BONDAGE." REMEMBERING WITH GRATITUDE THE REDEMPTION OF OUR ANCESTORS FROM EGYPT, REJOICING IN THE FRUITS OF OUR STRUGGLE FOR FREEDOM, WE LOOK NOW WITH HOPE TO THE CELEBRATION OF A FUTURE. WE PRAISE YOU, O GOD OF ALL EXISTENCE, WHO CREATES THE FRUIT OF THE VINE.

(All drink the second cup of wine.)

Continuity With the Past
L: Blessed are you, O Lord our God, who sanctified us and commanded us concerning the eating of bitter herbs. In Numbers we read, "They shall eat it with unleavened bread and bitter herbs." Matzah is unleavened bread baked in haste with no time for leavening. The moror are bitter herbs, symbolic of the bitterness of slavery and the misery of life in Egypt. For the Egyptians "made their lives bitter with hard labor in mortar and bricks and at all kinds of labor in the fields." (Ex 1:14) The haroset is a mixture of chopped fruit and spices which resembles the mortar the Israelites made in Egypt. Preserving a bond with the observance of our ancestors, we combine the Matzah, haroset, and moror (parsley) and eat them together.

C: TOGETHER THEY SHALL BE: THE BREAD OF FREEDOM, THE HERBS OF SLAVERY. FOR IN THE TIME OF FREEDOM, THERE IS KNOWLEDGE OF SERVITUDE AND IN THE TIME OF BONDAGE, THE HOPE OF REDEMPTION.

(Place all elements on the Matzah and eat together.)

Four Questions
Y: Why is this night different from all other nights? On all other nights, we eat leavened bread; on this night only Matzah. Why?

P: When Pharaoh let our ancestors go from Egypt, they had to flee in great haste. They packed their dough quickly and had no time to bake it. But the hot sun baked it into flat unleavened bread which they called "Matzah." To remember, we eat this kind of bread.

Y: On all other nights, we eat all kinds of herbs; on this night, we especially eat bitter herbs. Why?

P: Our ancestors were slaves in Egypt and their lives were made bitter. Not to forget their suffering, we eat bitter herbs on this night.

Y: On all other nights, we do not dip herbs at all; on this night we do. Why?

P: We dip the celery in salt water because it reminds us of the green that comes to life in the Springtime. We dip the bitter herb in haroset as a sign of hope. Our ancestors were able to suffer the bitterness of slavery because it was sweetened by the hope of freedom.

Y: On all other nights, we do not dine with special ceremony. Tonight we dine with special ceremony. Why?

P: To eat in leisure like this is a symbol of freedom. We eat like this to remind ourselves that on this night, many thousands of years ago, our ancestors were freed from slavery. I am glad that you asked these questions because, though the story is old, it is always new and we must repeat it every year, again, and again, that we may not forget the blessings of freedom. Let us then, tell the story of the Passover once again as it is found in Exodus 12:1-13; 21-34.

The Third Cup of Wine
(poured but do not drink yet)
L: Together we take the cup of wine, now recalling the third divine promise:

C: AS IT IS WRITTEN: "I WILL REDEEM YOU WITH AN OUTSTRETCHED ARM." WE PRAISE YOU, OUR GOD, GOD OF THE UNIVERSE, WHO HAS CREATED THE FRUIT OF THE VINE.

(All drink the third cup of wine.)

Four Questions
Y: Why is this night different from all other nights?

P: Tonight we celebrate the life of Jesus Christ, God's gift to us. *Read John 3:16-17.*

Y: Why is this night different from all other nights?

P: Tonight we celebrate God's gift to us of Shalom (Peace) and the Holy Spirit. Jesus said at the Last Supper: *Read John 14:15-17, 25-27.*

Y: Why is this night different from all other nights?

P: Tonight we celebrate God's gift of love shared between us, each to the other. Jesus gave us a new commandment. *Read John 15:12-17.*

(Continued on page 94)

Easter Acrostic

by Carolyn Egolf

How many words can you think of that begin with the letters of Easter? Begin by spelling EASTER vertically, and let students suggest as many words as they can that begin with each respective letter. Example:

- **E**—Eggs, Eternity
- **A**—Angel, Appearance
- **S**—Savior, Spring
- **T**—Trial, Trinity
- **E**—Ecstasy, Everlasting
- **R**—Risen, Resurrection

This activity lends itself well to all ages, and classes are usually amazed at how many words and ideas relate to the Easter theme. Words can simply be listed, or classes can be challenged to individually or collectively write phrases or formulate thoughts into poetry, as in this example:

E is for ETERNAL, a life that's ours to choose.
A is for the ANGELS—They told the Easter news!
S is for the SAVIOR, who death finally overcame;
T is for the TRINITY—God, three in one, the same.
E's for EVERLASTING, life that's free and new;
R's for RESURRECTION! May this bring great joy to you! ✝

Litany For Lent

by Carolyn Egolf

Leader 1: In this season of Lent, let us not only give up doubts and fears, but...

People: Let us give ourselves to hope and confidence.

Leader 2: "For God did not give us a spirit of timidity, but a spirit of power, of love and of self-discipline" (II Tim.1:7).

Leader 1: Let us not only give up gossip, judgmental thoughts, and comments about others, but...

People: Let us give ourselves to words of understanding and encouragement.

Leader 2: "A word aptly spoken is like apples of gold in settings of silver" (Prov. 25:11).

Leader 1: Let us not only give up grudges, resentments, and hurts, but...

People: Let us give ourselves to forgiveness, openness, and freedom.

Leader 2: "Be kind and compassionate to one another, forgiving each other, just as in Christ God forgave you" (Eph.4:32).

Leader 1: Let us not only give up busyness and frenzied living, but...

People: Let us give ourselves to service and productive living with calmness, order, and peace.

Leader 2: "Peace I leave with you; my peace I give you. I do not give as the world gives. Do not let your hearts be troubled and do not be afraid" (John 14:27).

Leader 1: Let us not only give up pessimism, cynicism, and discouragement, but...

People: Let us give ourselves to God's promises, comfort and encouragement.

Leader 2: "Through these he has given us his very great and precious promises, so that through them you may participate in the divine nature..." (II Pet. 1:4a)

All: Thanks be to God! ✝

Scriptures quoted are from New International Version Containing the New Testament and Psalms and Proverbs. Zondervan Bible Publishers, Grand Rapids, MI, 1991.

Infamous Traitor

by Joanne Wilson

Judas spearheading the greatest tragedy of history? Why? What were his motives?

Judas came from Kerioth, the only apostle not from Galilee. Judas was his Greek name, Judah, his Hebrew name. We are not told when Judas first met Jesus. It may have been when Jesus and his followers went to Judea. Jesus saw great potential in Judas or he would not have chosen him, evidenced in giving him charge over the money bag.

One of the following characteristics may have plunged him into betrayal:

AMBITION. Judas wanted Jesus to conform to the popular idea of the Messiah, overthrowing the Roman government and establishing an earthly kingdom. This would give Judas a high position. Realizing little chance of the earthly fulfillment of his dreams, his love of Jesus turned to hate. Ambition trampled love and honor.

GREED. After the anointing at Bethany Judas bargained for betraying Jesus. The sight of Mary's lavish sacrifice increased his resolve.

He bargained with the authorities for thirty pieces of silver. The desire for money blinded Judas to decency, honesty and honor. He didn't care how he got it.

Perhaps Jesus looked at Judas when he said, "Do not store up for yourselves treasures on earth...but treasures in heaven...for where your treasure is there your heart will be also. You can't serve God and wealth." Or another time when Jesus spoke to the disciples, "Whatever you have said in the dark will be heard in the light, and what you have whispered behind closed doors will be proclaimed from the housetops." (Luke 12:15) Jesus said, "Be on your guard against all kinds of greed; for one's life does not consist in the abundance of possessions." (Luke 12:15)

JEALOUSY. Judas may have been jealous of John, the Beloved Disciple. Jealousy can wreck a life. Judas in his self-centeredness wanted to be first.

HATRED. Some say Judas came to hate Jesus because Jesus knew his every thought and action. The sinless life of Jesus was a rebuke to him.

NATIONALISM. Possibly Judas was one of the dagger bearers, a band of violent nationalists, prepared to undertake assassination and murder to set Palestine free. Judas as a fanatical nationalist could have seen in Jesus his dreams of national power come true. Perhaps he plotted to join the apostles to further his nationalistic beliefs. When Jesus refused the way of power, Judas turned against Him in bitter disappointment and betrayal.

POWER SEEKER. Judas tried to force Jesus to use his power to save his own life and further act against the Romans. When Jesus was in power, Judas would be a big wheel. His plan went awry and in remorse Judas committed suicide. He was disappointed at the failure of Jesus to fulfil his expectations. Seeing Jesus heading toward the cross, Judas rebelled.

Judas refused to accept Jesus as he was. He never learned that it is not Jesus who must changed but he must be changed by Jesus. Judas refused to be changed even though Jesus gave him many opportunities.

MURDERER. Others say Judas joined the apostolic band with definite intention of betraying Jesus. Some seek to elevate Judas and his cowardly act to free him from the charge of motives and cowardly treachery. Some say Judas was a strong patriot seeing Jesus as an enemy therefore betrayed him in the interests of his country.

No one is sure which motive drove Judas to the dreadful act, perhaps a combination of motives. However, when we examine the words of Judas himself the greed motive seems well based. "Why was this perfume not sold for three hundred denarii and the money given to the poor?" Then the Scripture adds, "He said this not because he cared about the poor, but because he was a thief; he kept the common purse and used to steal what was put into it." (John 12:56) Judas also said, "What will you give me, if I betray him to you?" (Matthew 26:14-16) Later he confessed, "I have sinned by betraying innocent blood."

What did others say about Judas? John said, "He was

a thief." (John 12:6) Luke said, "Then Satan entered into Judas." (Luke 22:3)

Jesus said "...one of you is a devil." (John 6:70) At the last supper Jesus said, "...woe to that one by whom the Son of man is betrayed! It would have been better for that one not to have been born." (Matthew 26:24 NRSV).

Perhaps Timothy was thinking of Judas when he wrote, "For the love of money is a root of all kinds of evil and in their eagerness to be rich some have wandered away from the faith and pierced themselves with many pains." (1 Timothy 6:10)

Regardless of the motives Judas had, he was a rebel against God and his teachings. Selfishness carried him to the extreme, rejecting all spiritual values.

The Judas incident proves the freedom of the will. God never forces, He appeals in love. It shows God's foreknowledge and His sovereignty, using our choices (good or bad) for His own great purposes and plans. Judas was not a puppet, but responsible for his sin.

Jesus loved Judas even though he knew the betrayal plan. When Judas led the soldiers to the garden, Jesus called Judas "Friend." Jesus gave Judas the opportunity to repent.

Judas had the privilege of living for Christ but he chose to betray him, end his own life, and forever be remembered as the infamous traitor.

On this Good Friday, let us examine our own hearts. Are there any characteristics of Judas there—selfish ambition, greed, jealousy, or hatred?

Prayer: Dear Lord, help me deal with things in my life that are not pleasing to you. Help me be a faithful follower of yours, not a Judas. In Jesus' name. Amen. ☩

A Lenten Journey
(Continued from page 84)

do not like to think about those who betrayed, denied, mocked, and crucified him. Sometimes we are not unlike those who deserted Jesus. Today we place a crown of thorns on our Lenten cross to remind us that Jesus was crucified. Our journey of Lent ends with this crown of thorns. We wait in the darkness for God to come.

Easter Sunday

Hear these words from the writer of First Peter. *For you know what was paid to set you free from the worthless manner of life handed down from your ancestors. It was not something that can be destroyed, such as silver or gold; it was the costly sacrifice of Christ, who was like a lamb without defect or flaw. He had been chosen by God before the creation of the world and was revealed in these last days for your sake. Through him you believe in God, who raised him from death and gave him glory, and so your faith and hope are fixed on God.*

Last week our Lenten journey ended with Good Friday, with the death of God's chosen one, Jesus of Nazareth, on a cross. But our journey has not really ended, for today we celebrate a new journey that we are about to begin. God's power is greater than death itself. We are not Good Friday people. We are Easter people! Today we begin a new journey as God's Easter people and Christ goes before us. Today we place a butterfly on our Easter cross to remind us that like a caterpillar changes into a butterfly, we are changed too by the resurrection of Jesus the Christ! ☩

Good Friday Newspaper

by Deborah Payden

Create a newspaper that might have been printed on Good Friday in Jerusalem. This project is a good one during Lent for older elementary, middle or high school students. Such a project involves a variety of learning skills. In order to work on this project students will need to read and reflect on the passion narratives of Jesus, do research on the biblical time period, use language arts and drawing skills, use a computer (optional), learn about newspapers, work together on a project that has a deadline, and use their creative imaginations! Much of the work can be done during a regular study or meeting time. But some of it may have to be completed by students on their own. You may want to find adults in your church that can help "print" the newspaper by use of a computer, copy machine, etc. Use your imagination and the imaginations of the students! It is helpful if the teacher, or another adult serve as the Editor to make the final layout, and go over each article written. The completed newspaper can be given to church members on Palm Sunday. Or the paper can be sold and the proceeds used for a special mission project. Here is a sequence of activities during the six-week Lenten season to help in organizing this project.

1. **Introduce the Idea**
   - make a list of departments/type of articles in a newspaper (news, editorials, classified ads, obituaries, sports, home and garden, weather, crosswords, editorial cartoons, comics, business, etc.)
   - talk about the process/deadline/ assignments, etc.
   - introduce resource books for students to use in writing (Bible Dictionary, Commentaries, Bible Atlas, etc.)

2. **Read and Discuss Events of Holy Week** *(see end of article)*

3. **Make Assignments.**
   - discuss different ways to present these events in a newspaper (interview, commentary, editorials, etc.)
   - make assignments (one suggestion is that each person get a "serious" and a "fun" article or piece to work on for the paper.)
   - brainstorm ideas for name and possible logo for newspaper
   - set first deadline

4. **Check on Progress Each Week**
   - work during regular meeting time
   - make sure deadlines are met

5. **Make Final Deadline.**
   - Find someone to do final type and "set" newspaper
   - Make time to put newspaper together (staple, fold, etc.)
   - Decide how to "deliver" paper to congregation

6. **"Deliver" Newspaper on Palm Sunday.**

EVENTS OF HOLY WEEK

Palm Sunday—Mark 11:1-11; Matthew 21:1-9; Luke 18:35-43

In the Temple—Mark 11:15-19; Matthew 21:18-19; Luke 19:45-48; John 2:13-17

Anointed at Bethany—Matthew 26:6-13; Mark 14:3-9; John 12:1-8; Luke 7:36-50

Conspiracy to Kill Jesus—Matthew 26:1-4; Mark 14:1-2; Luke 22:1-2; John 11:47-53

Last Supper—Matthew 26:26-30; Mark 14:12-16; Luke 22:1-23; John 13:1-38

Betayal—Matthew 26:14-16; John 13:21-30; Mark 14:43-45; Luke 22:47-53

Arrest of Jesus—Matthew 26:47-56; Mark 14:43-52; Luke 22:47-53; John 18:2-11

Peter's Denial—John 18:25-27; Luke 22:54-62

Trial by Elders—John 18:28-19:16

Trial by Pilate—Luke 22:63-23:25; Mark 14:53-15:15; Matthew 26:57-27:31

Crucifixion—Matthew 27:32-61; Luke 23:26-55; Mark 15:21-47; John 19:17-42 ✞

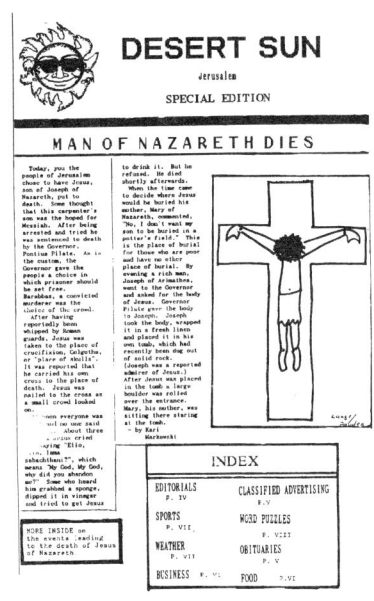

LENT: NOT DEATH BUT LIFE RENEWAL
(Continued from page 82)

Week 7: IT IS BEAUTIFUL

In the week after Easter it is important to have a closure celebration to the Lenten growth time. I suggest that you have some type of potluck party sharing in the goodness of what God has brought us, not only through creation but also in Jesus' resurrection from the dead. In this resurrection we see that Christ did for us what nature does every spring. Out of death comes life. Because Jesus died for us we are able to grow and enjoy the life of spring. At the end of the party it might be nice to give out seeds and tell the teens that Easter is not about ending but a new beginning. Invite them to plant the seeds so that the new life which Jesus gave us might be shared with others. Challenge them to plant the seeds for someone else or in a new place so that this Lenten growth will spread like the wind spreads the seeds. End the evening by reading John 17:24-26. ✞

LENTEN STEPS
(Continued from page 89)

Y: Why is this night different from all other nights?

P: Tonight we celebrate Jesus' gift of life that we might know God's forgiveness and receive life eternal. *Read Luke 22:14-20.*

The Last Supper
L: On the night that Jesus gave himself up for us, at a table with those who would desert him and deny him, he took bread, gave thanks, broke the bread, gave it to his disciples and said, "Take and eat, this is my body which is given for you. Do this in remembrance of me."

C: SEND YOUR POWER OF THE HOLY SPIRIT UPON US AND UPON THIS BREAD THAT WE MAY KNOW THE PRESENCE OF THE LIVING CHRIST, BE RENEWED AS HIS BODY, AND BE TRANSFORMED INTO HIS LIKENESS; FAITHFULLY SERVING HIM IN THE WORLD, AND LOOKING FORWARD TO HIS COMING IN FINAL VICTORY.

L: When the supper was over, Jesus took the cup, gave thanks to God, gave it to his disciples, and said, "Drink from this, all of you; for this is my blood of the new covenant, poured out for you and for many, for the forgiveness of sins." (Matthew 26:27c-28) We do this as often as we drink of it in remembrance of Jesus Christ. Using this cup, Jesus proclaimed that he was the Messiah and that the dawning of the Kingdom was here.

C: THROUGH HIM, WITH HIM, IN HIM, IN THE UNITY OF THE HOLY SPIRIT, ALL HONOR AND GLORY IS YOURS, ALMIGHTY GOD, NOW AND FOREVER. AMEN.

(*All eat a piece of Matzah and drink a fourth cup of wine.*)

(*Close with Jesus' prayer from John 17:1-26.*) ✞

*Taken from bulletin used by Bethel Lutheran Church, Phoenix, AZ

Easter Dawn Youth Service

by Dallas Brauninger

Prelude

Call To Worship: "The Empty Tomb"—1 John 20:1-18

We used this reading as an innovative way for the young people to enter the chancel. Encourage youth to speak with surprise in their voices as if it were the first time to hear the story.

Participants: 3 (individuals or small groups of readers)

(Readers 1 and 2 read from microphone in center aisle behind last filled pew.)

1: Early on the first day of the week, while it was still dark Mary Magdalene came to the tomb and saw that the stone had been removed from the tomb.

(Reader(s) 1 walks up to another microphone on left side in chancel.)

2: So she ran and went to Simon Peter and the other disciple, the one whom Jesus loved, and said to them, "They have taken the Lord out of the tomb, and we do not know where they have laid him."

(Reader(s) 2 joins 1 at microphone on left side of chancel while readers 3 and 4 walk to the microphone in the center aisle behind the last filled pew.)

1: Then Peter and the other disciple set out and went toward the tomb. The two were running together, but the other disciple outran Peter and reached the tomb first. He bent down to look in and saw the linen wrappings lying there, but he did not go in.

(Readers 3 and 4 stand behind center aisle microphone)

3: Then Simon Peter came, following him, and went into the tomb. He saw the linen wrappings lying there, and the cloth that had been on Jesus' head, not lying with the linen wrappings but rolled up in a place by itself.

(Reader 3 walks to assigned chair in chancel. Reader 4 reads from behind center aisle microphone then walks to assigned chair in chancel.)

4: Then the other disciple, who reached the tomb first, also went in, and he saw and believed; for as yet they did not understand the scripture, that he must rise from the dead. Then the disciples returned to their homes.

1: But Mary stood weeping outside the tomb. As she wept, she bent over to look at the tomb; and she saw two angels in white, sitting where the body of Jesus had been lying, one at the head and the other at the feet. They said to her, "Woman, why are you weeping?"

2: She said to them, "They have taken away my Lord, and I do not know where they have laid him."

1: When she said this, she turned around and saw Jesus standing there, but she did not know that it was Jesus.

(Reader(s) 5 walks in from front aisle to microphone at right front of sanctuary.)

5: Jesus said to her, "Woman, why are you weeping? Whom are you looking for?"

2: Supposing him to be the gardener, she said to him, "Sir, if you have carried him away, tell me where you have laid him, and I will take him away."

5: Jesus said to her, "Mary!"

2: She turned and said to him in Hebrew, "Rabbouni!"

1: (which means Teacher).

5: Jesus said to her, "Do not hold on to me, because I have not yet ascended to the Father. But go to my brothers and say to them, 'I am ascending to my Father and your Father, to my God and your God.' "

2: Mary Magdalene went and announced to the disciples, "I have seen the Lord"; and she told them that he had said these things to her.

Hymn: "Were You There?" (all verses)

Sunrise Reading: "Easter Morning"[2]

Cast of Characters:
  James, son of Zebedee
  John, brother of James
  Mary Magdalene
  Peter
  Jesus
  Roman Soldier

(Setting: Jerusalem, Easter Sunday monring. James and John are in hiding. Mary has just learned that Jesus has risen; Mary has told Peter and together they are trying to find James and John.)

John: Now what?

James: I'm not sure.

John: At least he was able to make a grand exit.

James: How can you say that? You were there—hiding in the crowd. You saw him cry in agony. You heard his cries to God. There was nothing fake about that. How can you say such a thing?

John: He was still able to make a grand exit. There, up on that cross, was righteous Jesus, being a good Jew by resisting the Romans to the end. He died a national hero—of sorts. However, the ones that he left behind, who had made real life investments in him, were the big losers.

John: You are going mad with grief, but I think I know what you are talking about. Brother Judas has already committed suicide and I'm afraid Peter might do the same any time.

James: Don't you realize we are all in danger? The Roman death squads are probably after us as well. Because of our dear Jesus, we are dead men. In faith we believe him; now he has taken our futures away from us.

(Crash and then silence. In the distance a ROMAN SOLDIER can be heard.)

Roman: Anyone who has knowledge regarding the whereabouts of the dead revolutionary, Jesus of Galilee, is bound by loyalty to Caesar to come forward immediately. All conspirators will be swiftly punished. Those who assist Rome will be well rewarded.

James: See, we are dead men. We have to leave Jerusalem tonight.

John: And go where? Back to Galilee? You know as well as I do that when we abandoned our father for Jesus we died in our father's eyes. You saw how he tore his coat when we threw our nets down. He has already adopted two of his workers to replace us.

James: Yes, I know that. When Jesus was alive, it didn't bother me that father had cut us off. Now with nothing else, I do feel betrayed. We've been conned.

(Another crash offstage)

John: The Romans must have found us. Quick, hide!

(James and John hide. Mary and Peter enter, gasping for breath.)

Mary: I saw him! He is alive!

Peter: Yes, yes!

Mary: James and John, come out of hiding. I know you are here. He is alive!

John: *(Still in hiding.)* What do you mean?

Peter: He is alive!

James: I saw the Romans thrust a spear in his side. He is as dead as can be.

John: James is right. I was hiding in the same place and saw the same thing.

Mary: Yes...No! I mean to say that he was dead, but now he is alive. It is a miracle. It's just as he said.

Peter, John, and James: What?

Mary: That he would rise on the third day...and he did. His mother and I went to the tomb this morning. The Romans had sealed the tomb with a huge boulder, but when we got there, the boulder had been rolled away. We found his wrappings inside the tomb, but not his body. He's alive.

John: You must have entered the wrong tomb.

Peter: No she didn't. She helped lay our Lord to rest, after all. *(Remorseful)* God knows I should have been there to bury him, but I was afraid.

James: A missing body does not mean he is alive, though I wish he were. Unfortunately, this merely means that those Romans are making sport with our Lord's body. Come John, we must go to the fortress and resuce his body.

(James and John move as if to go, but Mary restrains them.)

Mary: For once in your lives, you could let me finish my story. I saw him.

John: What do you mean by that?

Mary: He talked to me.

Peter: Jesus told Mary to tell us—and all his followers—that he is alive and that he will be with us always.

John: That's crazy! You're both insane!

(Jesus enters)

Jesus: Peace brothers. Peace sister Mary. It is good to be with you again.

James, John, and Peter: Oh! Dear Lord! Thank God!

Jesus: Get up, rejoice and tell everyone that I am alive! You have mourned enough over my death. Start rejoicing. Here, as a sign of my love for you, take this bread and remember that God's love cannot be defeated. Here, take this cup and be empowered by the spirit of God. *(Shares bread and cup with them.)* Now full authority in heaven and on earth has been committed to me. Fo forth, therefore, and make all nations my disciples; baptize people in the name of the Father, the Son, and the Holy Spirit. Teach them to observe what I have commanded you. And be assured that I am with you always—to the end of time.

(Jesus vanishes)

James, John and Peter: He's gone.

Mary: Don't worry. Didn't you hear him? He will be with us always. Come let us tell the others. Let us tell everyone that our Lord lives!

All: Jesus, our Lord, has risen! Praise God! *(All exit praising God and proclaiming the good news.)*

Hymn: "Jesus Christ Is Risen Today" (Vs. 1 & 4)

Offertory

Doxology

The Prayer Of Our Savior

Prayer Litany:

Before the service, ask the youths to jot down phrases about what Easter means to them, what they are grateful for at Eastertime, what Easter teaches them and how their lives are changed because of Easter. Compile their responses into a prayer litany such as that below:

L: Easter is about new life. Easter is about being with family. Easter reminds us that these things are special:

P: Family, freedom, pets, car, individuality.

L: At Easter, we thank You, God, because You:

P: Love us and You gave Your son for us.

L: Easter teaches us this about Jesus, the cross and Resurrection:

P: To have faith and that there is always hope.

L: Easter makes this difference in our life:

P: Our freedom from death, that is, life after death.

L: Because of Easter morning,

P: I will try harder to be kind to somebody I am not compatable with.

L: Because of Easter morning,

P: I will try harder to look on the bright side and to find happiness there.

ALL: Hear our prayers, God, in Jesus' name, Amen.

Closing Hymn: "Up From The Grave He Arose" (3 Verses)

Benediction: "Praise God" from Psalm 150[3]

Use with eight teams of two or more readers. If you do not have this many youths, let each pair add two successive lines before moving down the center aisle. Each team of readers comes down the chancel steps and stands at the base to read their section. Then that team goes down the center aisle or side aisles to the back of the church.

ALL: Praise God in this sanctuary;

1: Praise God!

2: Praise the Creator in this mighty firmament!

3: Praise God for mighty deeds; Praise God according to His surpassing greatness!

4: Praise God with trumpet sound;

5: Praise God with lute and harp!

6: Praise God with tambourine and dance;

7: Praise God with strings and pipe!

8: Praise God with clanging cymbals;

ALL: Praise God with loud clashing cymbals! Let everything that breathes praise our God! Praise God!

Postlude

(Please join us in the gathering room for Easter breakfast.) ☦

---

[1] Adapted from Easter 2, Psalm 150 in Brauninger, In the Beginning Was the Word: Scriptures for the Lectionary Speaking Choir, Cycle B (Lima, Ohio: C.S.S. Publishing Co., Inc., 1993).

[2] "Easter Morning" by John Mansell. Henry R. Rust, Ed., Celebrating Holy Week (Prescott, AZ: Educational Ministries, Inc., 1993), pages 96-97.

[3] Adapted from Easter 2, Psalm 150 in Brauninger, In the Beginning Was the Word: Scriptures for the Lectionary Speaking Choir, Cycle A (Lima, Ohio: C.S.S. Publishing Co., Inc., 1992).

Resurrection Rap

by Deborah Payden

Rap is simply words put to rhythm and rhyme. Here is one that tells the resurrection story. Our youth used it in worship as a way of sharing the story in a contemporary art form. Both children and youth enjoy rap.

Alleluia, Alleluia, Alleluia, Amen;
Alleluia, Alleluia, Alleluia, Amen;
Now all was dark and all was bleak,
When after the Sabbath, the first of the week,
Sister Mary of Magdala to the tomb did go,
To care for the Lord, with oil and so.
She thought and she wondered about that old stone,
And how she would move it when all alone.
The guards were asleep and no help at all,
Mary just kept walking on up to that wall.
Surprise, surprise, the cave was clear,
So Mary ran away with fright and fear.
"Brother Peter", she said, "They've taken the Lord."
"Sister Mary," spoke he, "You're out of your gourd."
So Peter and all went back for a look,
No Jesus was there, in any cranny or nook.
There lay on the stone a cloth of bright white,
It gave some disciples there now quite a fright.
But the savior's words, some others knew,
He had surely been risen now, that was true.
The angel of the Lord, said, "Fear not, dear friends
For Christ is risen, this isn't the end!"
Brothers and sisters, hear the news today,
The power of death, God has put away.
Rejoice and sing praise the world is new!
Christ has led us on the Way, and the Way is true.
So spread the good news to far and wide,
   We too like Christ shall be glorified!
   Alleluia, Alleluia, Alleluia, Amen,
   ALLELUIA, ALLELUIA, ALLELUIA, AMEN! ✝

Personalities Of The Passion

by Carolyn Egolf

Jesus—Matt. 26-28; Mark 14-16; Luke 22-24; John 18-21
Peter—Luke 22:54-62; John 18:15-27
Judas—Luke 22:3-6; 47-53; John 18:2-7
John—John 19:25-27
Mary (mother of Jesus)—John 19:25-27
Pilate—John 18:28-19:16
Thomas—John 20:24-29
Angels—Luke 24:1-11; Mark 16:5-8
Thief—Luke 23:32-43
Mary Magdalene—John 20:1-3, 11-18
Joseph of Arimathea & Nicodemus—Mark 15:42-47
Two on the road to Emmaus—Luke 24:13-34

Choose one of the above and respond to the following questions:

1. Why did you choose this particular person?
2. Would you like to have been this person? Why or why not?
3. What did the person do in the Holy Week/Resurrection scenario?
4. How did the person feel? Suggest several possible emotions or feelings.
5. Write a poem, letter, monologue, series of questions, or other expression regarding the experience of the person you've chosen.

Youth will find this exercise valuable in getting into the feelings of people central to the Easter story. Too often we study only at the surface level and fail to realize the impact of oly Week events on the persons who lived those events. ✝

Lenten Feelings

by Joanne Wilson

Overview of Sessions

Theme of the Series: Feelings in the Lenten season biblical account.

Scripture: Lenten experiences in the four Gospels.

Goal of the Series: To equip students with skills needed to handle uncomfortable feelings so they can mature, have fun, and enjoy life while building worthwhile relationships.

Methods of the Series: Using questions, discussions, and role-play. Designed to invite a response which personalizes the concept and applies it to daily life.

LESSON 1: *Rejection*
Objective: To teach that Jesus knows the feeling of rejection and wants to help believers through rejection experiences
Scripture: Mark 15:16-20; Luke 23:18-21; Psalm 56:34
Theme: Handling rejection

LESSON 2: *Anger*
Objective: To teach that angry feelings come to everyone but we can control our reactions with God's help
Scripture: Matthew 27:22-26; James 1:19-26
Theme: Handling anger

LESSON 3: *Jealousy*
Objective: To identify jealousy and find ways to handle it
Scripture: Matthew 27:15-18; Mark 15:10, Galatians 5:26
Theme: Handling jealousy

LESSON 4: *Failure*
Objective: To teach that failure can be overcome with God's help
Scripture: Acts 12:12, 25; 13:5, 13-14; 15:37-39; 1 Corinthians 15:57-58
Theme: Handling failure

LESSON 5: *Love*
Objective: To teach the true meaning of love by examining the love of God in the crucifixion
Scripture: John 3:14-18; 10:14-18; 15:12-13,17
Theme: Giving and responding to love

LESSON 6: *Review*
Objective: To reinforce the previous five lessons through review
Scripture: 2 Timothy 3:10-17
Theme: Handling feelings in review

Suggested conclusion to the study: Give each student a copy of What You Should Know About Lent and About Easter, inexpensive booklets purchased from A Scriptographic Booklet by Channing L. Bete Co. Inc. South Deerfield, MA 01373, 1-800-628-7733.

BIBLIOGRAPHY

Berger, Terry. I Have Feelings, Human Sciences.
Devault, M. Vere. Psychology, Steck-Vaughn Co..
Johns, Richard. Return to Heroism, Doubleday.
Kalb, Jonah and Viscott, David. What Every Kid Should Know, Houghton.
LeShan, Eda. What Makes Me Feel This Way? Macmillan.
Odor, Ruth Shannon. Moods and Emotions, Child's World.
Splaver, Sarah. Your Personality and You, Julian Messner.
Wilt, Joy. Handling Your Ups and Downs, Weekly Reader Book.
Wilt, Joy. Needing Each Other, Weekly Reader Book.

What You Should Know About Lent, Channing L. Bete Co.

About Easter, Channing L. Bete Co.

LESSON 1: REJECTION

Preparation: Make copies of instructions for groups and scramble letters of the word REJECTION on the chalkboard.

Introduction: Feelings exert a powerful force in life. (Ask for common kinds of feelings.) Feelings affect the body, causing a stomachache or "butterflies" when you face a test in school. Feelings affect thinking. They determine reactions to people and situations. Feelings form attitudes. The ability to handle feelings determines character, reputation, and even future jobs and family life. These lessons will help us learn about feelings and how to handle them. We can't help feelings that come, but we are responsible for reactions to them.

The events that surrounded the crucifixion, created different feelings, or emotions. What feelings do you think Jesus had, surrounding the events of Palm Sunday, Maundy Thursday, and Easter? (Brainstorm words: Suffering, denial, sadness, cruelty, injustice.) Can you unscramble the feeling word on the chalkboard?

No one likes to be rejected; felt left out, ignored, belittled, criticized or ridiculed. Rejection hurts.

Group Work: Divide into groups of 2 or 3. Allow 15 minutes for discussion. (Answers need not be written. Information in parentheses is for the leader.)

Instructions:
1. Read the Scripture listed below.
2. What was Jesus' reaction in each situation?
4. Make up a skit of a present day rejection with the right way to handle it.

Scripture:
1. Matthew 12:9-10; 13-15. (Jesus was rejected for doing good. He healed the man with the withered hand. Pharisees plotted to kill him. Jesus departed.)

2. Luke 4:16, 21, 29-30. (The message Jesus delivered in the synagogue was rejected. Jesus left.)

3. Luke 22:41-43. (Jesus prayed about his rejection experience. Angels strengthened him.)

4. Luke 22:47-51. (Jesus was betrayed by Judas, a disciple. Jesus healed an ear. He returned good for evil.)

5. Luke 22:54, 63-65. (Jesus was beaten by soldiers. It's implied that Jesus said or did nothing.)

6. Luke 23:6, 9. (Herod questioned Jesus. Jesus was silent.)

Share Discoveries: Reassemble groups. Share group discoveries and skits.

Leader: Jesus was rejected but not defeated. We can be victorious through rejection also. Give suggested helps in handling rejection. (Guidelines should come from the students. Make copies of these guidelines and distribute them next week.)

Suggestions For The Leader:
1. Be yourself. Don't act in a way that is not comfortable or right, just to be popular.

2. Realize that everyone is rejected some time in their life. Sometime we are rejected because we serve God. Sometimes we need to improve our character.

3. Cultivate Christian friends.

4. Face the facts. Are you good company, a good sport, easy to be with? If you're the problem, admit it and look for ways to improve.

5. Think of Jesus. He knows how you feel. Jesus will never reject those who have dedicated their life to him. Jesus cares for you no matter how others treat you.

6. Accept the fact that everyone will not like you.

7. Forgive those who reject you. It may take time, but you can do it with God's help.

8. Remember, no one is useless to God. He has a plan for your life. You're valuable. God made you. He loves you.

9. Seek help from Scripture and a Christian friend.

10. Pray for endurance and determination to serve God.

Conclusion: Feelings are a big part of everyday life. As you live for God, the Holy Spirit will help you react in a positive way. It's a lifelong challenge. Rejection will come. With God's help we can be victorious. Enjoy the best life possible. Watch out for those feelings!

Closing Prayer: Dear God, Thank You for the Lenten season. Help us to remember that You will help us in times of rejection. In Jesus name. Amen.

LESSON 2: ANGER

Preparation: Prepare written instructions. Have ready a pan of water with a lid.

Introduction: The events surrounding the crucifixion, created different feelings, or emotions. (Review rejection.)

Listen as these verses are read to discover another feeling. Read together Matthew 27:22-26; Mark 15:12-14; John 19:46.

(Fill a pan with water. Put on the lid.) When I put this pan on the stove and turn the burner on high what happens? (Water will boil over if not watched.)

Anger resembles pressure inside, like a pan of boiling water. Anger builds and builds, then spills out over everyone. Take off the lid or turn off the heat, the water stops boiling.

You can't keep angry feeling from coming, but you can do something about your reactions to them. A big step in growing up is learning to control inside feelings and reacting to them in an acceptable way.

What is the difference between instant anger and simmering anger? Selfish anger and unselfish anger? What causes anger? Give examples of anger you have experienced. Helps for the leader:
- INSTANT ANGER flares up like a match but quickly dies.
- SIMMERING ANGER lasts a long time.
- SELFISH ANGER says, "I'm mad because I didn't get my way." Jesus never demonstrated selfish anger.
- UNSELFISH ANGER is strong feelings about mistreatment and sin against God and His people. Jesus expressed unselfish anger when he chased the money changers from the temple.

Group Work: Divide the students into four groups:

Instructions:
Group 1: Read this poem. How is it true to life? Give it a title. Add another verse.

When I'm disappointed
Or things don't go my way;
I get so very angry
And hateful words I say.

My words come out in bunches,
They cut and slash and tear;
They hurt all those around me
As though I didn't care.

Sometimes my fist starts punching
And at another aim;
Then later I'm so sorry;
I hang my head in shame.

I'm asking God to help me;
To live for Him each day.
He promised He would teach me,
To live the Christian way.

Group 2: What causes anger? Formulate ways to relieve the pressure of anger.

(Loss of homework, guilt from unwise actions, family problems, rejection by a friend, unkind words, continually pushing for better grades, responsibilities beyond physical or mental ability, disappointment, failed plans, etc.)

Group 3: What are the physically, mentally, socially, and spiritually affects of anger?

Anger causes changes in the body. More sugar and adrenaline pour into the blood stream. The heart pumps faster, blood pressure rises, muscles tense.

Failure to recognize and understand our anger may lead to health problems, such as, high blood pressure, heart problems, headaches, stomachaches, skin disorders, constipation, diarrhea and obesity. Repressed anger causes accidents and hurts relationships, destruction of property, abuse, violent behavior, and even murder.)

Groups 4: What should you do when someone is angry with you?

Suggestions: Ways To Relieve The Pressure Of Anger
- Identify the cause.
- Calm down before speaking. Shouting makes it worse.
- Listen carefully to the other side.
- Express feelings clearly without insulting remarks.
- Negotiate and compromise.
- Seek help from a friend.
- Be active (jogging, running, bike riding, hobbies)
- Get enough sleep.
- Explain feelings to a friend or speak aloud to God.
- Remember, God allows us to go through hard experiences to teach us and help us grow.

- God will forgive when asked. Forgive others.

- Apologize for wrong actions. However, your attempt to make things right may be rejected.

- If no agreement can be made, walk away.

WHEN OTHERS ARE ANGRY WITH YOU:

- Remember angry people say things they don't mean.
- Listen carefully to what is said.
- Consider the cause.
- Forgive.

Group Discoveries: Reassemble the groups and share

Conclusion: Read James 1:19-26.

Closing Prayer: Dear God. Help us learn to react to anger in a way that pleases You. In Jesus' name. Amen.

LESSON 3: JEALOUSY

Preparation: Write two Bible references on the chalkboard: Matthew 27:15-18. Mark 15:10. Draw eight short lines on the chalkboard, one for each letter of the word "jealousy." The word "envy" is used in place of "jealousy" in some versions.

Introduction: Read the guidelines developed for handling rejection and anger in lesson 1 and 2.

We avoid feelings that make us uncomfortable. We often repress hurtful feelings. This is unhealthy. If hurtful feelings are not dealt with, they hinder a person from growing and living a healthy and happy life.

The first step in handling uncomfortable feelings is to identify them. Then they are more easily resolved.

Lesson three deals with another feeling. The word can be spelled on the lines on the board. (Take turns guessing a letter for each line, until the word is completed.) Read Matthew 27:15-20 and Mark 15:10 to find out who had this feeling toward Jesus, preceding his arrest in the Garden of Gethsemane. (Chief priests.) Why were these religious leaders jealous? Many of the people were following Jesus instead of the chief priests. Jesus was healing people and getting more attention than they were.)

Define and discuss the word jealousy.

Group Work: Divide into groups of 2 or 3.

Group 1: Tommy's sister made the Honor Roll, but he didn't. Describe Tommy's feelings. Make up a skit of the best way to handle this situation. Describe the reaction to jealousy in Genesis 26:14.

Group 2: Mary entered the poetry contest. Her friend Pat *won* a blue ribbon. Mary didn't. Make up a skit of the best way to handle this situation. Describe the reaction to jealousy in Genesis 37:11.

Group 3: Tom and his friend, Ted, practiced hard for the softball team tryouts. Ted made the team but Tom didn't. Make up a skit showing the best way to handle this situation. Describe jealousy in Numbers 16:3.

Group 4: Jill was sure her friend, Nancy, would choose her as the partner on the school science project. Nancy chose the new girl instead. Make up a skit showing the best way to handle this situation. Describe the jealousy in Daniel 6:4.

Group 5: Betty wanted a new dress for the party. Her father said work was slow and he couldn't buy her a dress. Betty's friend, Jodie, bought the dress Betty wanted. Make up a skit showing the best way to handle this situation. Describe the jealousy in Matthew 27:18.

Group Discoveries: Reassemble to share discoveries and skit.

Work together formulating ways to handle jealousy. Ask a volunteer to record and post the guidelines. Guidelines should come from the students. Make copies of the guidelines for distribution next week.

Suggestions:
- Poor ways to handle jealousy:
  - Say mean words
  - Yell and scream
  - Plot revenge
  - Try to compete with them
  - Compare yourself with others

- Good ways to handle jealousy:
  - Admit you are jealous.
  - Remember you are a special person.
  - Remember you can do many things that the other person cannot.
  - Keep your mind busy on a hobby or project.
  - Get involved with people.
  - Tell God how you feel.
  - Talk to an understanding adult.

Conclusion: Everyone is jealous some time in their life, some more than others. Remember that you are a special person to God.

Read James 1:19-26. To be slow to anger is good advice. Anger gives the impression of hatred, dislike, and contempt. Stubborn resistance is the usual reaction to anger. Anger does more harm than good.

Closing Prayer: Dear God, Thank You for loving me. Help me to remember that I am special to You. Help me react in the right way to jealousy. In Jesus' name. Amen.

LESSON 4: FAILURE

Preparation: Print one letter of the word "failure" on seven pieces of 8 1/2 x 11" paper, Mix the letters and give them to the first seven people arriving.

Background For The Leader: Judas was a failure as an apostle, an example we must not follow. Jesus did not reject him nor did he expose him as a traitor, but he knew the intent of Judas.

Suicide is high on the list of causes of death among American youth, emphasizing the importance of this lesson. The Lenten feeling of failure which led to suicide is discussed, but do not dwell on suicide at length. Focus attention on the positive life of Mark who overcame failure and made a lasting contribution to humanity, the book of Mark in the New Testament.

His Roman name was Mark and his Jewish name was John, sometimes called John Mark. He lived in Jerusalem with his mother, Mary (not the mother of Jesus). Nothing is recorded about his father. Mark's home was a meeting place for the Christians. Peter went there when the angel released him from prison.

When Paul and Mark's uncle, Barnabas, went on their first missionary journey, Mark went along as their helper. When plans were made to cross the Taurus mountains, Mark headed back home to Jerusalem. We do not know why. He failed as a missionary helper.

Later Mark wanted to go with Paul and Barnabas on the second missionary journey. Paul refused to take him. The disagreement separated the two men. Paul took Silas in place of Barnabas. The results of Mark's earlier failure were still affecting him.

We do not know how Mark handled his failure but we know he didn't give up. Later he wrote the Gospel of Mark. When Paul was in prison, he asked Mark to visit him.

Introduction: The events surrounding the crucifixion, created different feelings. We discussed and developed guidelines for handling rejection, anger, and jealousy. (Read the Guidelines from each of the preceding three lessons.)

Today we are looking for another feeling in the crucifixion story. (Ask the seven people with letters to come to the front. Ask volunteers to rearrange people with a letter to spell a feeling word.) The feeling is failure. (Read Matthew 27:15 together.) Who failed? (Judas).

Jesus chose Judas, knowing his ability in business and in planning and handling money. Judas did not live up to his potential. He could not handle failure.

A young man in the Bible by the name of Mark also failed, but he did not let it ruin his life. We are going to learn about him and develop a plan for handling failure.

Group Work: Divide into groups of three or four people.

Instructions: Have you ever failed? Describe the feeling of failure. How did you handle that feeling?

Learn about John Mark by reading the Scripture verses Acts 12:12,25: 13:5,13-14; 15:37-39; Colossians 4:10; 2 Timothy 4:11; Philemon 24; 1 Peter 5:13.

Write one or more suggestions that will help when failure comes.

Groups Discoveries: Reassemble groups and share discoveries.

Suggestions:
1. Ask yourself: What can I do about it? What can I learn from this experience?

2. Talk to God about it. (If you have let God down, ask His forgiveness. Failure does not make us forever useless.)

3. Let it out. (Tears help wash away the hurt inside. Holding the hurt inside sometimes causes stomachache, headache, or bad dreams.)

4. Talk to a good listener.

5. Get busy. (Read a book, play a game, visit a friend, help someone.)

6. Read the Bible and pray.

Conclusion: Failure does not make us useless. Remember Mark. Read 1 Corinthians 15:51-58.

Closing Prayer: Dear God. It's no fun being a failure. Help me overcome failure and be useful to You and others. In Jesus' name. Amen.

LESSON 5: LOVE

Preparation: Write LOVE IS on the chalkboard.

Instructions: The words in parenthesis are for the leader only. Provide poster board and colored markers for each student.

Introduction: Review guidelines from the preceding lessons.

Group Work: Divide into three groups. Appoint a leader for each group. Distribute the instructions.

Instructions:
Group 1: Read John 3:14-18. What feeling of God is shown? What do these verses tell us about God's love? How does God show His love to us today? (Jesus shows us God's love.)

Group 2: Read John 10:14-18. What feeling of God is shown? What makes you think God loves you? How is God's love revealed to you? (God loved us so much that He gave His Son to die for us . The Bible tells us of God's love.)

Group 3: Read John 15:12-13,17. What feeling of God is shown? What is our responsibility? Suggest ways that you can show love to others. (God has given us His Word to show us how to love others.)

Sharing Discoveries: Reassemble the groups and give answers to the questions. How are these verses connected to the Lenten season?

Brainstorm: Call out words that could be added to the words LOVE IS.

Suggestions:
- Love is calling a person by name.
- Love is looking in their faces.
- Love is listening without interrupting.
- Love is helping people with life problems.
- Love is giving an encouraging word.
- Love is a smile or a friendly nod.
- Love is a word of praise or thanks.
- Love allows an honest expression of feelings.
- Love offers understanding without criticism.
- Love never embarrasses.
- Love is feeling cared for.
- Love is being valued by others.
- Love makes you feel accepted, liked, and respected.
- Love makes you feel safe.
- Love makes you feel happy.

To be loved you must:

1. Love yourself. God created you and loves you, this makes you special, therefore you should love yourself.

2. Love others. God created them and loves them, this makes them special also. Because they are special people, created and loved by God, you should love them too.

The love of God is a source of strength. A close relationship with God produces a love for others. How do events of the Lenten season show us how Jesus showed God's love to us?

When we love God we will do what He tells us in His word. This will give the right direction to our lives.

To love God is a solid foundation on which to build a life. The more we love God, the greater the effect will be on our character and actions.

God's love provides a plan for mending broken relationships caused by sin.

Poster Project: Distribute poster board and markers. Use words and pictures to express the word LOVE.

Sharing Creations: Post pictures around the room. Ask students to explain their thoughts behind their posters.

Conclusion: God's word makes it very clear that He loves us. Say John 3:16 in unison. Loving and giving are a part of God's plan for everyone. When we grow up giving and receiving love, we will live healthy and exciting lives.

Think of ways you will show your thanks for God's love this week. Direct a period of silent prayer for each student to express thanks to God.

Turn to John 3:16 and I John 4:8. Read both verses in unison.

Closing Prayer: Dear God, thank You for the love You showed us through the life and death of Jesus. Help me receive this love every day through reading the Bible and prayer. Help me love others as Jesus did when he was here on earth. In Jesus' name. Amen.

LESSON 6: REVIEW

Preparation: Place slips of paper and pencils on the table. Label a large grocery bag LENTEN FEELINGS and place it near the table. Write JESUS, CROWD, LEADERS, JUDAS, MARK, and JEWISH LEADERS, on six slips of paper and drop them in the bag. Place five containers labeled REJECTION, ANGER, FAILURE, JEALOUSY, and LOVE on the table. Using the guidelines developed in the last five lessons, cut the guideline paper into two guidelines each and drop them in the bag.

Write these directions on the chalkboard for early arrivals: Write a guideline, a verse, or an event from the Lenten season. Write as many as you have time for. Extra paper is on the table. Drop your paper in the LENTEN FEELINGS bag.

Introduction: Divide the students into nine groups. Take turns, each reading a verse from 1 Corinthians 15:18, 57-58. Repeat verse 57 together after verse 58 is read. Lead a discussion with these questions: What do verse 57 and 58 mean? How does it apply to the Lenten season. How does it apply to the feelings we have been talking about in the last five lessons?

We have many different feelings. We talked about five of them evident in the Lenten happenings. (Read each label on the containers.)

Pass the bag for students to take out a paper. Take turns reading the papers, then placing them in one of the labeled containers. Student must give a reason for their decision. Accept any reasonable explanation.

Conclusion: Feelings controlled by Bible teachings result in growth and happiness as a Christian. Uncontrolled feelings cause unhappiness. We are learning to balance feelings with determination and discipline to follow the will of God.

Learning to handle feelings is a big part of growing up. Babies cry to get their own way. Insisting on your own way is an uncontrolled baby feeling. Mature people think more and more about others. Mature people feel good about themselves in their handling of feelings.

First, ask yourself these questions. What is this feeling? Why do I have this feeling? What can I do about it?

Secondly, talk about it. Tell God about it. Take a walk, voicing aloud your feelings to God. Talk to a Christian adult.

Third, find a way to release the pressure built up inside by bad feelings. Everyone is different. One way will work for you and not for someone else. Run, pound a pillow, work on your hobby, visit a friend, help someone. Keep busy! Continually nurturing a bad feeling makes it worse.

Saturate your mind with Scripture. Read it. Study it. Memorize it. Attend church and Sunday school determined to listen, learn, and grow.

Read Paul's charge to Timothy, 2 Timothy 3:10-17. What do these verse mean to you? What is Paul's challenge to his readers? (To be loyal to the Word of God.) How is the Bible useful? (Teaching, reproof, correction, and training.) Studying the Scriptures can make you useful to God and to people around you.

Closing Prayer: Dear God, Thank You for reminding me of various feelings of the Lenten season. Help me to react to my feelings in an acceptable way. In Jesus' name. Amen.

Projects: Make a list of projects suggested by the class. Vote for one class project or ask each person to choose one they will complete by themselves or with one other person.

Suggestions:
1. Take a trip to the library to borrow books on feelings.
2. Invite a pastor or psychologist to speak on feelings.
3. Look for video tapes dealing with feelings.
4. Write and produce a play about feelings.
5. Write a poem about feelings.
6. Divide the students into 5 groups, each making a poster of the guidelines developed for one of the five feelings.
7. Make a chart listing different feelings. For a week, place a check mark at the feelings you experienced. Evaluate your reactions to them. ☦

Back To Jerusalem

by Carolyn Egolf

Host: "Welcome to "Back to Jerusalem." Modern technology allows us to do things once thought impossible, and tonight we are privileged to go back in time to Jerusalem to interview some of the key personalities in the Easter story—the Easter drama if you will. We've chosen to speak with Judas, Peter, and Pilate, asking all the same questions, namely:

- Tell us about yourself, your occupation, background, and interests.
- How did you feel about Jesus?
- The third question will be personalized regarding what each one did in relation to Jesus.
- What happened afterward; in other words, how was your life changed?
- What advice do you have for believers in the 1990's?

INTERVIEW WITH JUDAS

Host: Judas, welcome to our program. You've gotten bad press over the years. Tell us about yourself.

Judas: Yes. I'd like the chance to defend myself. I was an upstanding citizen, a capable one at that. It pleased me when I was selected to serve as treasurer for the disciples. Generous people supported us, and I kept accurate records, watching carefully how funds were dispersed. Remember how I questioned the ointment (perfume) being so lavishly poured on Jesus, suggesting it could better be spent on the poor? I was as mindful of human need as anyone. I'm really not a bad fellow.

Host: Tell us the how you felt about Jesus.

Judas: How did I feel about Jesus? I loved the man with filial love—the kind one has for a dear friend or brother. I admired and respected him and was constantly amazed at how he sensed what individuals needed and met those needs. Remember I gave three of the best years of my life to be with him and really anticipated being part of his leadership team when he became the earthly King of the Jews.

Host: Why then did you betray him?

Judas: Why did I betray him? Some people say I had no choice—that my role was set in a Divine plan, and if I hadn't betrayed him someone else would have. I don't know about that, but I do know that something had to happen. We were at what you could call the crossroads or the breaking point—at least it seemed so to me. So many were believing in and following Jesus. Remember the way he was celebrated on Palm Sunday when he rode into Jerusalem? You would say he was "riding the crest of popular opinion," and it seemed to me the time had come for the Big Move—making him King, so he could save us from the ugly Roman control, heavy taxes, and constant haranguing. Not only were the Romans oppressing us, but those Pharisees and other religious leaders were constantly testing him, cornering him, and attempting to entrap him. I felt it was time to act, but never in my wildest thoughts did I dream he would be killed—crucified...Oh, the memory of that realization...

Host: That gives us a clearer understanding of you, Judas. What happened then?

Judas: Once I realized that Jesus was not going to pull off another miracle and save himself, I also realized that my hopes and dreams of helping him in his earthly kingdom were lost. What did 30 pieces of silver mean now to me, him, or anyone? I scurried back to the Pharisees to cancel the deal, and you can only begin to imagine my humiliation at that time. When they didn't accept my apology or make any effort to help me undo my wrong, I suddenly felt desperate, trapped, like a crazed animal in a cage, with nowhere to go, no one to care, nothing to live for. If Jesus was going to die, so was I—soon and fast. Everything became a blur, and I ended my life quickly.

Host: Judas, yours is a story of noble plans gone awry—of dreams that died. What would you say to people in the 1990's with dashed hopes and broken dreams?

Judas: Obviously, I'm not one from whom folks might be inclined to learn, but let me suggest two things:

1. Be gentle with people; try to understand. Too many make surface judgments. Motives may be purer than they appear. Mine were, but no one would listen.

2. Give God time. My actions were due to haste; I wanted to hurry the Kingdom, and because I tried to hasten the process, I lost my chance to be part of it.

Host: Thank you, Judas. We feel we know you better than we did, and hopefully we can learn from your experience.

Scriptures related to Judas: Matt. 26:14-16 Matt. 27:3-10; Luke 22:3-6; John 12:1-8

INTERVIEW WITH PETER

Host: Our next guest is Peter, known also as Cephas, or "The Rock." Tell us about yourself, Peter. We understand you were a fisherman by trade—part of a family business.

Peter: Yes, my brother John and I were in business with our dad, Zebedee. Mind you, it was a prosperous business, and we assumed some day it would be ours. The work was hard, but there was always adventure and the thrill of the catch, you know. Then along came Jesus, and there was something so captivating about him, so winsome, that when he said, "Follow me, and I will make you fishers of men," we left everything immediately and became his most intimate companions.

Host: How did you feel about Jesus?

Peter: Feel about him? It's hard to put into words, though I'm not known for lack of words. Usually I'm first with the questions, first with the answers, and first with an idea or solution. I suppose my feelings can best be expressed as tremendous admiration; maybe it would be called brotherly love. Yes, I think love is not too strong a word. I respected him, but continued to find him mysterious. Just when I thought I understood the man and his message, something would happen, and I'd have to work out a new understanding.

Take, for example, the transfiguration. That was quite an experience—one I shall never forget. The light was so dazzling. Jesus was in the center with Moses on one side and Elijah on the other; some say that was to symbolize Jesus' uniting the law and the prophets. It was a time so worthy of remembering that I quickly suggested we build three tents or tabernacles to commemorate the event. But no—that was not to be, and all too soon the event was over, and we were back to the day-to-day ministry. Day-to-day isn't quite right, as no two days were the same. Every one was adventurous and different.

You probably have heard too about the time I tried to walk on the water. Jesus was walking toward us on the water. Mind you, this is not a figment of imagination. It really happened. I jumped out of the boat, and for a few moments I walked on water too! It was glorious! But then, I realized what I was doing, lost my confidence and began to sink. Jesus pinpointed my problem immediately, saying, "O man of little faith, why did you doubt?" (Matt. 14:31b). Talk about humiliation—I felt like a first-class failure! I wanted to be such a champion for Jesus and blew it more often than I care to remember.

Host: That's a perfect lead-in for our next question. Why did you deny one you admired so much?

Peter: Ah, such a bitter memory. I wish I could blot that terrible night from my memory forever. . .I cringe every time I realize that I'm remembered as the one who denied his Master, and yet, given the same situation, the same darkness, the same setting, most everyone in the audience would have done the same.

We'd had supper with Jesus; it was Passover time you remember. He'd talked about new meanings for the Bread and Wine, something about his body and blood. He'd washed our feet. I didn't like that part at all till he explained, or at least tried to explain what he meant about greatness and servanthood. We still didn't "get it." It was too much to understand, though I guess he'd been trying for three years to teach us those lessons.

Host: What happened then?

Peter: After supper, we went to the Garden of Gethsemane. We were so tired, and even though Jesus asked us to watch with him, James, John, and I fell asleep. Three times we drifted off. Jesus was so sad in the garden, as if something he dreaded was about to happen.

Host: What happened then?

Peter: Once Judas and the soldiers came and took Jesus, we were scared. We scattered like sheep! Despite my fear, I was curious, as well as concerned about Jesus, that I came close enough to see what was happening, and hopefully distant enough not to be seen. But. . .I was seen and questioned about my relationship to Jesus. Three times someone thought I was part of his group. One even said my accent betrayed me. I was so scared. How would you feel when the One who'd worked all kind of miracles was led meekly away in chains to face beating, trials, and who knows what? If he couldn't or wouldn't save himself, I could see myself next in line for the same treatment. The desire for self-preservation is unbelievably strong, and at that point, I wasn't ready to die—at least not if I could help it. After I'd denied three times that I knew Jesus, the cock crowed. Jesus had predicted exactly that, and once I realized how well he knew me, I "went out and wept bitterly." I should say that is the very worst memory of my life. Men like me don't cry easily, you know.

Host: How was your life changed?

Peter: So much happened so fast. Easter morning was unbelievable; you remember John and I raced to the tomb. He got there first, but I charged in right away. Typical me—blundering right in! When we realized Jesus was alive, our happiness knew no bounds!

That scene on the shore, though, when he fixed breakfast for us and asked me three times if I loved him still puzzles me sometimes. Three times—once for each time I said I didn't know him—he asked if I loved him and told me to "Feed my sheep." There isn't time to relate all that happened, but Pentecost when three thousand were converted by my sermon was exhilarating! The days of the early church—oh, such challenge and adventure! If you read my two epistles, you'll see that I mellowed much over the years, and am a much more settled and secure Peter near the end of my life than the Peter you met in the gospels.

Host: Your story has so many facets upon which we've barely touched. Tell us now what advice you have for modern Christians.

Peter: My first advice is to think first; speak and act later. Most of my mistakes were due to my impetuous nature. Careful thought, sensible words, and gentler actions would have saved me from many downfalls. I give this advice to individuals and to churches.

Secondly, know human weakness, yours and others. The Greeks put it simply, "Know thyself." Again if you understand your own personality, your weaknesses, and your strengths, you'll be more aware of your probable areas of failure and be more understanding of others when they make mistakes or fail to live up to your expectations. Finally, never underestimate what God can do with you. If you look at Scripture, both Old and New Testaments, you'll see that God didn't choose super people to do His work. He chose very unlikely people and strengthened them for particular assignments. Can you imagine a temperamental, impetuous, blundering one like me doing miracles, helping to found the early church, and writing epistles that have strengthened believers for centuries? No, never, never underestimate what God can do with a committed life.

Scriptures related to Peter: Matt. 25:26-46; Matthew 16:69-75; Matt. 17:1-8; Matt. 14:25-33; John 13:5-20; John 20:1-10; John 21:9-18; Acts 2:14-42.

INTERVIEW WITH PILATE

Host: Pilate, you're like Judas in that you've gotten bad press over the years, and many fault you for not changing the course of history when for a time, albeit brief, you in fact, seemed to have that power. Tell us about yourself.

Pilate: You have to remember I was part of the political web of the time. Rome was in power, and we were given areas to rule at the whim of the officials in Rome. Galilee was known as a beautiful, but nasty area to rule because of the religious fanaticism there. Believe me, I was not thrilled to be appointed governor of Galilee. Jews were contrary and were always wearying the people with their many religious rules to remember. Then there was Jesus, who was becoming more popular by the day, as he taught and healed the multitudes. I was caught between the power of Rome, who controlled my job and in a sense my life, these Galileans who were forever either rebelling or looking for a Savior, and the Jews who constantly mixed politics and religion.

Host: How did you feel about Jesus?

Pilate: My philosophy about Jesus was "Live and let live." As long as he didn't bother me or upset the political process, I didn't really care what the people thought of him. After all, it was Rome I had to please. No one would admire me anyway since I represented Rome and its power to tax, to punish, to conscript, and do all the other things oppressive governments do to people.

Actually regarding Jesus, I rather admired him. He never spoke ill of anyone, always seemed to do good, and even though the people spoke about a king, there seemed nothing that threatening about him. Even when he came to trial in my court, I felt deep down that he was innocent. Even the religious leaders couldn't agree on the charges, and when you have false witnesses in the courtroom, it's anybody's guess as to guilt or innocence of the accused.

Host: Why did you bow so readily to the will of the people?

Pilate: Don't say I bowed so readily. Didn't you sense the frustration in my question, "What is truth?" That was deep soul-searching, and every thinking person asks that question at sometime during his life—many times, for that matter.

Then there was my wife's dream. Remember she said I should have nothing to do with Jesus? Now I'm no believer in dreams, signs, and that stuff, but my wife is a serious-minded person, and her counsel has saved me more than once. I just couldn't believe the pressure of the people. I thought sure I could appease them by freeing Barabbas. They'd want him crucified; he was a killer, you know, and Jesus would be freed. But mob psychology ruled the day,

(Continued on page 110)

The Pretzel

by Christie L. Jenkins

Pretzels are not usually thought of as having anything to do with religion. Long before they became a common snack food and their religious origins were forgotten they were associated with Lent. At a time when people prayed by crossing their arms over their chests, pretzels were shaped to represent this gesture and were meant as a reminder to people that Lent was a time of prayer.

The first pretzels were probably made by monks in Italy sometime during the 400's (the earliest known picture of a pretzel appears in a 5th century Vatican manuscript. They were made with only flour, water, and salt since any animal products such as eggs, fat, and milk were forbidden during Lent. They were called bracellae in Latin which means "little arms".

In time the pretzel found its way to Germany where it was known as a Brezel or Prezel. In Europe during the Middle Ages, pretzel vendors would begin selling their wares on Ash Wednesday. This custom of selling pretzels only during Lent lasted up until the last century. To this day in some European countries the 4th Sunday of Lent is known as Pretzel Sunday.

Children were also given pretzels as a reward for learning their prayers. And today's youth might be interested in the following.

Make pretzels using a flour/cornstarch clay (these are obviously not to be eaten). Make different size pretzels. Smaller ones can be put on a string and worn. Or glue a piece of magnetic tape to the back of the smaller ones to make refrigerator magnets. Larger ones can be made to be used as paperweights. Using paint, decorate these pretzels with symbols of prayer or with Bible verses having to do with prayer.

Youth groups might use this project as a way to raise money for some worthy cause. Giving alms is also an ancient Lenten custom.

Another project would be to bake contemporary pretzels. Using a recipe for edible pretzels, shape the dough to represent the gestures people now use when they pray. Be creative. How could the dough be shaped to represent these gestures of prayer?

Pretzels, the traditional and contemporary, might be served during the coffee hour during Lent. ✟

Back To Jerusalem
(Continued from page 118)

and when they yelled, "Crucify!" they meant Jesus! I still can't believe that crowd's reaction. It was almost as if they were out of control and no longer thinking. No one came to Jesus' defense, and he wouldn't defend himself, so I literally washed my hands of the whole affair. Remember my job and likely my life were on the line at this time.

Host: What happened afterward?

Pilate: You do have to give me credit for the strength I did show. After Jesus was crucified, the leaders still weren't satisfied, and like tattling children came saying, "The sign says 'King of the Jews.' " They wanted me to have it rewritten. Instead I responded firmly, "What I have written, I have written." Deep in my heart, I knew Jesus was innocent, and I believed and still believe He was the Messiah. Oh, how I wish I had shown more courage when it would have mattered.

Host: What advice do you have for us?

Pilate: I'd say first of all to study and search. The eternal question "What is Truth?" begs for answer by every person in every generation. Study the Scriptures, study your world, and be aware. Had I known more about the prophecies, more about the people, and more about their needs, I'd have been much better prepared to face both Jesus and the crowds.

Secondly, stand for what you know to be right. I tried, but my efforts were too little, too late. My conscience was partially appeased, but regret is a terrible thing to live with. While standing for truth is often costly, cowardice has a dear price. I know. I've paid for a lifetime...

Host: There you have it friends. Voices from Jerusalem. We trust you've gained new insights into the lives and motives of those who lived Holy Week. We trust you've been challenged to examination of your own lives and motives. ✝

Scriptures related to Pilate: Matt. 27:1-2, 15-27; John 18:28-19:22.

Readings For Lent
(Continued from page 49)

reading for Sundays (or a prayer and meditation) so you will have a devotion for each day between Ash Wednesday and Easter.

2. Prepare the materials to be given to the writers. Put the date the material is to be read, the title of the reading, and the citation to the Bible at the top of a worksheet. It is not necessary to copy the scripture. Leave the rest of the sheet blank.

3. Give the assignments to the writers. Ask each participant to write a meditation on the scripture listed at the top of the page. This should either be typed or handwritten in fine-point permanent marker ON THE WORKSHEET so that you may reproduce the material by a copy machine.

4. Set a time by which the materials must be completed. Be sure to allow adequate time to collect late meditations and to collate and reproduce the material. The project coordinator should select a title, design a cover, and may wish to write a dedication or foreword for the booklet. The materials can be reproduced on a copy machine or may be typed and taken to a print shop if a more finished (but more expensive) booklet is desired. Distribute the booklets so they will be available to your congregation by the beginning of Lent. ✝

LENTEN PUZZLER
(Continued from page 70)

ABOUT THE AUTHORS

TERESA BAGGOT is a fourth-grade catechist at St. James Catholic Church in Solana Beach, CA, and she works part-time for St. Mary's Press of Winona, MN.

ANN BATEMAN is a certified Director of C.E. and a Diaconal Minister in the United Methodist Church, who lives in Salem, OR.

LINDA BLOOMGREN is a free-lance writer who lives in Minneapolis, MN.

DALLAS BRAUNINGER is a UCC minister and free-lance writer residing in Friend, NE.

H. MICHAEL BREWER is the pastor of a Presbyterian church in northern Kentucky.

ROBERT DAVIDSON is editor and publisher of **CHURCH EDUCATOR** and **CHURCH WORSHIP**, monthly publications produced by Educational Ministries, Inc. He is author of several books published by that firm, located in Prescott, AZ.

TERRY DEFFENBAUGH is a Catholic priest who specializes in youth retreats. He is author of several youth books published by Educational Ministries, Inc., including Come Watch with Me. He resides in Olympia Fields, IL.

JOYCE DeTONIE-HILL is pastor of Dimondale UMC in Dimondale, MI.

GWEN DRAKE is pastor of Jason Lee UMC in Salem, OR.

CAROLYN EGOLF is a free-lance writer living in Northumberland, PA.

VIRGINIA FLEISHANS from Mesa, AZ, is a free-lance writer.

SUSAN GREGG-SCHROEDER is a United Methodist minister in San Diego, CA.

DELIA HALVERSON writes for the United Methodist Publishing House and has been active in Christian education for many years. She is the author of several books and resides in Ft. Myers, FL.

DON HARTMAN is pastor of Zion UCC in Troy, MO.

ELLEN HUMBERT is a free-lance writer living in Mesa, AZ.

CHRISTIE JENKINS is a free-lance writer who resides in Northridge, CA.

DENISE KREBS writes the *Noah's Ark* column each month in **CHURCH EDUCATOR**. She is active in the parish where her husband is pastor in the Reformed Church of America. They live in Glendale, AZ.

PENNY LOWES is an active member of the First Congregational Church in Rochester, MI.

JANE MAEHR presently teaches kindergarten in west metropolitan Detroit. She has taught in Lutheran schools, trained preschool and elementary teachers, taught overseas, and served as a DCE in a UCC congregation.

CAROLYN MC DOWELL works with the Ministry of Music and Drama at Decatur First UMC in Decatur, GA.

PETER OLSEN is Minister of Education at the First Protestant Church, UCC, in New Braunfels, TX.

DEBORAH PAYDEN is Associate Minister at First Congregational Church in S. Milwaukee, WI.

MIRIAM PERRY is a free-lance writer from Phoenix, AZ.

MARY JO SHANNON is active in the Christian education program at Raleigh Court Presbyterian Church in Roanoke, VA. She is author of A Christmas Gift-Making Workshop (Educational Ministries, Inc.).

MAREN TIRABASSI is a free-lance writer and imterim minister living in Portsmouth, NH. She co-authored with Ruth Duck Touch Holiness (Pilgrim Press).

DAVID TREMBLEY is co-pastor with his wife of Broken Walls Christian Community in MIlwaukee, WI. They co-authored the Drama in the Church series (Educational Ministries, Inc.).

ELAINE WARD is the author of over 20 books published by Educational Ministries, Inc., her latest being Living with Jesus and the Book of Job During Lent. She resides in Austin, TX, and is a regular contributor to both **CHURCH EDUCATOR** and **CHURCH WORSHIP**.

ANN WIGGINS is a Christian educator in Tuscaloosa, AL.

JOANNE WILSON is a free-lance writer living in Northumberland, PA.